The Shape of
Texas

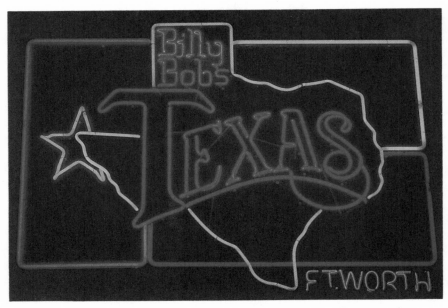

Billy Bob's billboard-sized neon sign, a registered logo, integrates several messages about Texas history and geography, conveying a sense of Lone Star patriotism, geographic expansiveness, and action. (Courtesy Billy Bob's, Fort Worth, Texas)

The Shape of Texas

Maps as Metaphors

RICHARD V. FRANCAVIGLIA

TEXAS A&M UNIVERSITY PRESS
COLLEGE STATION

The paper used in this book meets the minimum
requirements of the American National Standard
for Permanence of Paper for Printed Library
Materials, Z39.48-1984.
Binding materials have been chosen for durability.
∞

Library of Congress Cataloging-in-Publication Data

Francaviglia, Richard V.
    The shape of Texas : maps as metaphors.
       p. cm.
    Includes bibliographical references and index.
    ISBN 0-89096-664-8
    1. Texas—Popular culture—Maps. 2. Texas—Maps, mental.
3. Texas—History—Maps. I. Title.
G1371.E64F7 1995 <G&M>
912.764—dc20   95-18635
                                              CIP
                                            MAP

TO ELLEN,
WHO IS ALWAYS THERE

Contents

Acknowledgments

THIS BOOK COULD NOT HAVE BEEN WRITTEN WITHOUT THE HELP OF MANY people who enthusiastically brought "Tex-maps" to my attention. I especially want to thank colleagues at the University of Texas at Arlington (UTA): Gerald Saxon, Sally Gross, and Katherine Goodwin of UTA Special Collections; Profs. Ken Philp and Dennis Reinhartz and administrative assistant Nancy Whitted of the History Department; Kirsten Dennis and Darlene McAllister of the UTA Center for Greater Southwestern Studies and the History of Cartography; Karl Petruso of the College of Liberal Arts; Donna Darovich of the News Service; Jan Swearingen of the Graduate School of Humanities; and numerous students, including Jerry Stafford and Phil Schwartz, who shared many examples of Texas maps. UTA research assistant David Filewood helped locate Texas map graphics in telephone book Yellow Pages and city directories while serving as my research assistant. Gary Honeycutt of Texas Instruments (TI) provided information about the development of the TI logo. Carol Williams, curator of the Cattleman's Museum in Fort Worth, Texas, kindly researched Texas-shaped cattle brands, and popular culture authority Margaret King of Philadelphia located several Texas-shaped products and advertisements marketed on the East Coast. Scholar of popular culture Blanche Linden-Ward of Watertown, Massachusetts, called to my attention Texas maps in David Byrne's film *True Stories*. Anne Dingus enthusiastically reported on the Texas map project in an issue of *Texas Monthly* magazine; Dwayne Humphrey of Hughes Simulation Systems in Arlington helped with the aerial photography by ably serving as my pilot; Richard García and Gail Wood provided information about Fiesta Texas in San Antonio; Angela Enright of the Four Seasons Resort and Club arranged to have the Cottonwood Valley golf course illustration prepared; curator of collections Mildred G. Walker and the staff at the Dr Pepper Museum in Waco, Texas, assisted in locating early Texas maps in soft drink advertising. Monument dealer Ron Henry of Fort Worth described the process by which Texas maps have been created in stone; and Pam Minick, marketing director of Billy Bob's, provided a photograph of the company's distinctive sign. Debbie

Tallant of the Fort Worth office and Charles Ahner of Saint Louis, attorney for Southwestern Bell Yellow Pages, helped me secure permission to reprint Texas maps. W. Ross Moore Jr. alerted me to the Texas- shaped tree planting in Midland; and Doug Jones of the Superconducting Super Collider in Waxahachie provided photographs. Jim Steely of the Texas Historical Commission (THC) in Austin provided important information about the use of the Texas map on the THC seal. Stephen Shackelford of the Texas Department of Transportation in Austin provided information on the standardization of the Texas map. Randy Brown of KRLD in Dallas made available the artwork of the radio station's logo. Bob Donahue and Frank Jiménez of KMOL-TV in San Antonio provided photographs of the station's distinctive Texas map banner. David McDavid of Irving kindly provided graphics of his company's striking Texas branding iron advertisement, and Dick Meyer of Western Oregon State College alerted me to Texas-shaped images on the AIDS memorial quilt. Fellow cultural geographer Terry Jordan offered encouraging advice and reprints of important articles on early Texas and Texas identity. David Farmer, director of the DeGolyer Library at Southern Methodist University in Dallas, provided access to important materials, as did his helpful staff members.

Writing this book involved my entire family. My daughter, Heather, ever on the lookout for Texas-shaped items, sent me several. My wife, Ellen, patiently typed many drafts of this manuscript and provided numerous editorial suggestions. My son, Damien, was the first person to read the draft manuscript; his critique from the perspective of a college anthropology student helped ensure the manuscript's readability.

I am especially thankful for the financial assistance provided by the Summerlee Foundation of Dallas, which enabled many of these illustrations to be printed in color for the benefit and enjoyment of the reader.

In subtitling this book "Maps as Metaphors," I gratefully acknowledge the pioneering works of geographer Roger Downs, who authored a seminal *Professional Geographer* article with a similar title, which is cited in this text.

The Shape of
Texas

Introduction

FORT WORTH, TEXAS, HAS BEEN CALLED THE TEXAS MOST CITY BECAUSE IT IS so typical of the Lone Star State.[1] In the 1990s, tourism has emerged as one of Texas' largest industries, and visitors to Fort Worth are drawn to the historic Stockyards, where the city's image as a cattle and ranching center is "themed" into a lively tourist package that includes honky-tonks, gift shops, restaurants, historical exhibits, livestock shows, and rodeos. One of the Stockyards' biggest and most popular attractions, Billy Bob's, offers a dazzling country-western nightspot experience. Tourists are guided to the Stockyards district by Billy Bob's huge neon sign, which serves as an icon for modern Texas (frontispiece). Billy Bob's sign transforms a huge map of Texas—which has become America's most recognizable state outline—into a Texas flag by using a star blazing in the western portion of the state.

Significantly, Billy Bob's sign is red, white, and blue and connotes patriotism and a flamboyant expansiveness that has become part of Texas' image. Design experts recognize that this sign embodies action. The lettering style is flowing, conveying motion; the map outline is a bold shape that has curves, points, and angles; the star is radiant and bursting with energy. The sign is a metaphor for the new Texas, which is to say, it plays on a sense of history and action that is important for generating tourism and an image of the Lone Star State to the world.

Billy Bob's creative use of the map of Texas is not unusual or coincidental. The fundamental design element of Billy Bob's sign—the Texas map—is ubiquitous. No other single icon so readily identifies the state. Tourists visiting the gift shops at the Stockyards (and across the state) are greeted by a variety of "Texas kitsch" in the shape of the state—earrings, wristwatches, belt buckles, barbed wire ornaments, cutting boards, ice cube trays, serving bowls . . . the list is endless.

The map of Texas is part of the state's touristic landscape. Travelers approaching the Texas Panhandle city of Amarillo become aware of the Big Texan Motel, which uses a huge sign that flashes a series of messages in incandescent lights. One Big Texan message tempts the traveler to try a seventy-two-ounce steak—which is free to the person who can eat it all in less than an hour. Another message invites the traveler to swim in the motel's "Texas shaped pool" as the map of Texas appears illuminated on the huge sign (fig. I-1). Once lured to the motel, travelers indeed find a distinctive Texas-shaped swimming pool (fig. I-2) in which they can swim from El Paso to Houston, or from Amarillo to Dallas in a lesson in recreational geography.

Such uses of the map of Texas form an important part of Texas culture. Those who spend any time in the state soon realize that the map is used widely. It appears in both popular commercial and official uses: in the advertising of automobile repair shops, insurance agencies, restaurants (fig. I-3), and a myriad of government-related services, such as on car titles, license plates, highway signs ("DWI—You Can't Afford It"), on the badges and automobiles of many municipal police departments, and at state automobile safety inspection stations. Even food items such as pasta and tortilla chips in the shape of Texas are consumed, and Texans lounge in Texas-shaped hot tubs and some even swim in their own Texas-shaped swimming pools. Texans in search of a suntan can adorn themselves with small Texas-shaped stickers that, when removed, reveal the shape of Texas on untanned skin.

In the 1990s, what I call "Tex-map mania" has become a major fad.[2] From television station logos to landscaped areas along public rights-of-way, from T-shirt logos to jewelry, Texans are experiencing the map of their state in an unprecedented manner. Although many Texans find the use of the map quite "natural" (that is, it has become so common that many claim not to be consciously aware of it anymore), visitors may be overwhelmed by the profusion of Texas-shaped images. How can a map have such wide appeal—and such wide usage? It seems to be everywhere.

The Texas map even worked its way into Ann Landers' nationally syndicated column. "Perplexed in Pisa," an American military man overseas, wrote that his girlfriend became upset at his suggestion that, rather than giving her a diamond engagement ring, he buy some land in Texas and "have an expensive gold band made and attach to it a small charm in the shape of Texas . . . as a reminder of a wise investment."[3] Ann was as unimpressed as the girlfriend, however, and replied, "If you want to give her a little charm in the shape of Texas, it would make a nice Valentine's Day present."[4] That a charm in the shape of Texas was even being discussed at all is a tribute to the popularity of the map of Texas.

If Texans were a tribe located in an exotic part of the world, anthropologists probably would have seriously studied their peculiar use of the map by now. But as of this writing, no one else has described the phenomenon of Tex-map mania that is treated in this book. Although the phenomenon is peculiar to advertising and promotion of Texas products and services, it has become national and even international in scope. The map of Texas is found

FIG. I-1. This illuminated sign on Interstate Highway 40 east of Amarillo informs travelers that a Texas-shaped swimming pool awaits them at the Big Texan—a large, western-themed motel complex. (1991 photo by author)

FIG. I-2. The Texas-shaped swimming pool at the Big Texan Motel provides a lesson in recreational geography; the tired traveler can swim laps between El Paso and Houston. (1991 photo by author)

on a range of widely marketed products that convey a Texas identity. Consider, for example, Cincinnati-based Kroger Company's Texas Style baked beans, which are marketed nationally. The can's label features a map of Texas that seemingly reaffirms the authenticity of the product (fig. I-4). Avis Rent-a-Car also has used a portion of the map in a national magazine to advertise "Savings As Big As Texas" on its West Texas rentals. The map of Texas has been exported internationally by several Texas-based companies, among them

FIG. I-3. A restaurant in Hamilton, Texas, uses a Texas map to advertise cuisine familiar to the region. (1991 photo by author)

FIG. I-4. Marketed nationally in 1991, this product's label uses both words and graphic images to convey and authenticate its vaguely ethnic culinary tradition. (Photo by author)

Texas Instruments of Richardson (Dallas). As the European or African user of a Texas Instruments calculator interacts with this piece of high technology, he or she becomes aware of a small but intriguing symbol—the map of Texas—affixed to the product.

This book is dedicated to the iconic use of the map of Texas—that is, its use as a popular symbol, or metaphor, for the Texas identity. The subject of why and how maps are used as symbols has been studied very little. Maps, we have all been taught, are primarily designed to communicate information about location: they help us find our way or reaffirm ownership. When we consult a road map of Texas to find out how to get from one place to another, or to determine the location of a particular place or feature, such as the Alamo, we are using the map as tradition has taught us. Tex-map mania, as we shall see, goes beyond this. The map becomes an icon or symbol for Texas in the public mind. Although most maps serve quite practical—i.e., navigational or locational—purposes, only rarely do they become symbols, as, for example, when a resource conservation organization uses a map or image of the globe or earth to imply concern for or stewardship of those resources, or when a paint company like Sherwin-Williams advertises (as early as 1910) that its paint "covers the earth." Much the same thing happens when Billy Bob's uses a map of Texas to convey the image of a place that is associated with country-western music (in the *Urban Cowboy* tradition), ranching, an independent past as a republic (1836–45), and many other things. The map becomes a symbol for traditions and events and, perhaps, a symbol for Texas' western or southwestern location. Therefore, we cannot interpret the map of Texas as symbol unless we understand the myriad of images it conveys. Some (like ranches) are based on visual images; others (like size) are more abstract concepts.

This book, then, lies at the peculiar interface between cartography, graphics, popular culture, environmental perception, advertising, and historical geography. In it I shall answer several important questions about maps and about Texas' identity:

> 1. *What* is it about the map of Texas that lends itself to widespread use, and how does it relate to a wide range of other visual symbols of the state (such as the Lone Star, longhorns, armadillos, oil wells, and the Alamo)?
>
> 2. *Why* has the shape of Texas been adopted and utilized in a variety of ways, from personalized and vernacular imagery to a wide range of products and services that are marketed nationally and even internationally?
>
> 3. *How* did the map of Texas develop into the geographic form or outline we so easily recognize as "marketing" the state's identity?

4. *When* did the map of Texas become popular as an icon and does its popularity coincide with other developments in Texas (and American) culture?

5. *Who* recognizes and uses the map of Texas? Is its use associated with any particular sector of Texas society, or is it used and appreciated by all Texans?

The Texas map phenomenon is a subject of immense importance in part because it sheds light on the design integrity of images that are developed into consumable symbols; that is, it can help us understand how the process of popular culture works. The methodology of historians and art historians may help social scientists develop new ways of seeing and interpreting the visual environment of material culture.

In this book, the Texas map will be interpreted as a cartographic design that has been created in the context of the culture. Some readers may appreciate the maps illustrated and some may not, but whether one approves of the phenomenon of the Texas map's popularity is not important. Tex-map mania is a fact of life; therefore, I shall treat the symbols or icons as statements about Texas that must be interpreted outside of issues of "good" or "bad" taste and aesthetics. Some of these maps are whimsical, idiosyncratic, and engaging (fig. I-5), whereas others become rather standardized or businesslike when seen repeatedly (fig. I-6); nevertheless, all Texas-shaped images make important statements about Texas and Texans.

Readers will soon discover that Tex-map mania is inextricably linked to Texans' pride in their state and that I have a deep respect for the nearly legendary appreciation that we Texans feel for the state's mythic and real history. This loyalty to Texas is itself a phenomenon worthy of comment, and it certainly forms part of the character of Texans—and their image of themselves. In this book loyalty to Texas and the flourishing of the Texas map as a symbol are shown to be interrelated and inseparable.

This book, then, deals with a visible manifestation of a popular symbol that evokes a wide range of emotions—from humor when it is used in a clever or heavy-handed fashion, to patriotism when it is used seriously. The text is meant to be read as a narrative for the visual graphic materials. The reader will find more than one hundred map images of Texas illustrated and described, but these are only a portion of the thousands of maps one sees across the state. My personal collection contains more than one thousand Texas-shaped items, from campaign buttons to pasta. I hope I have selected examples that represent the range of Texas maps and that I have interpreted their meaning in the context of cultural history. Although most of the maps illustrated in this book are two-dimensional representations printed on paper, many maps are actually three-dimensional objects (ashtrays, jewelry, pencils, and utensils) that are part of what anthropologists and cultural

FIG. I-5. This distinctive 1983 advertisement transforms the Texas map into a smiling face complete with a cowboy hat. (Reproduced with permission of Southwestern Bell Yellow Pages, Inc.; all rights reserved)

FIG. I-6. Some images become more significant when seen in large numbers over a period of time, as is the case with automobile dealer Bill McDavid's logo—a small, gleaming Texas map that abounds on the trunk lids of automobiles. (1991 photo by author)

FIG. I-7. A Texas-shaped pencil is part of the extensive "Tex kitsch" market, a reminder that map images have become part of our material and popular culture. (Photo by author)

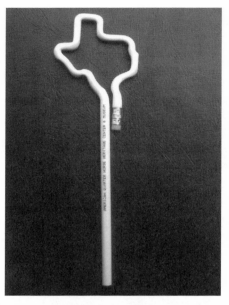

FIG. I-8. As part of the streetscape graphics in Poth, a small town in South Texas, the map is used to identify an enterprise and give a sense of place in a sprawling state that encompasses several major cultural regions. (1993 photo by author)

historians call "material culture" (fig. I-7). Like many tangible items, they can, and should, be interpreted as important artifacts that can tell us much about the way people view the world.

As a geographer, I have a special interest in the cultural landscape, which is a complex collection of artifacts. Thus, I have attempted to explain how the map image of Texas has become part of the signage (fig. I-8) and even the actual design of the landscape throughout the state. One soon realizes that Texas maps are not simply maps, but part of the way Texans visualize—and give order to—space and how they create images of place in the process.

The Shape of Texas treats a subject that is in its infancy, and so I remind, and warn, the reader that it represents the first serious attempt to interpret popular cartography; therefore, it must—by nature—be interdisciplinary and venture into territory at the edges of established academic thought where images and words become concepts and symbols.

1.
Maps and Identity

We don't get our image of the world from running around and looking at the world. We get it from some diagram or map.
— Thomas Saarinen, quoted by Richard Monastersky, "The Warped World of Mental Maps"

THIS BOOK IS ABOUT THE PROCESS BY WHICH MAPS BECOME POPULAR SYMBOLS. What we call a map—a representation, usually on a flat surface, of the whole or part of an area—can vary greatly in design, form, and content. Some maps are highly detailed, while others are so simplified that only a minimum of information is provided. For the most part, this book is about the simplest of maps, that is, those that depict only the basic shape of a geographic unit. However, even these simplest of maps can serve important purposes; in fact, as we shall see, the simplest of maps may serve most effectively in helping us recognize places that have unique positions in our minds or what some might call our national psyche.

If we were to search for, and collect, maps that depict only form (or shape) rather than distributions (or content), we would wind up with three types that illustrate basic cartographic techniques:

1. **Outline maps** (fig. 1-1*a*) are probably the most common. They simply consist of a line that describes the perimeter of a geographic entity, such as a continent or state. The outline can be scrawled in pencil or rendered in the most sophisticated neon, but it achieves the purpose of enclosing a geographic shape. The outline, or perimeter, may contain several recognizable forms, such as angles or curves, and it may somewhat simplify reality by reducing details. Nevertheless, the outline does more than enclose empty space. By giving definition to the outside, it encourages us to define the inside or interior as a place of possibilities. Outline maps invite us subconsciously to ask questions about what lies within the boundaries. What is the name of the mapped area? Are there other important

FIG. 1-1. Texas as depicted in three basic types of maps: (a) outline; (b) silhouette; (c) highlight or relief. (Graphic by author)

places or features (cities or rivers, for example) within it? This is why the outline map is so effective as a teaching tool: it forces us to recognize a place by its perimeter only—and then to add more geographic information from memory or even imagination.

2. **Silhouette maps** (fig. 1-1*b*) are more than simply a variation of outline maps, for they emphasize the massing or interior form rather than the perimeter of a geographic place. In their reliance on positive and negative lighting (that is, the concept of light and darkness) or color intensity (stronger or weaker colors), they emphasize the form and massing while reaffirming the outline. Whether the mapped area is lighter or darker than the background (that is, black on white or white on black) matters less than the contrast between the mapped area and the background. However, even though a bright (or white) mapped area on a dark background invites the placement of some information (content) within the map, the ultimate purpose of silhouette mapping is impact. The geographic shape or form dominates as it leaps from the background. Silhouette maps, then, would seem to depict geographic relationships by isolating the mapped area in space and making it stand out from its background (much as a bright star stands out in a black void). And yet, by isolating the image, they also reaffirm that it does have a position in the context of space.

3. **Highlighted (or relief) maps** (fig. 1-1*c*) emphasize the interplay between light and shadow. This technique provides a three-dimensional aspect to the mapped area, for one sees part of the perimeter or outline of a map accentuated by shading, as if the mapped area were solid and a light were thrown across it from, say, top to bottom (or north to south). Highlighted maps may be considered a variation of the outline map, for they certainly give us information about the perimeter. Highlighted maps show only the outline by inference, however. Such maps are visually complex, for they manipulate, and rely on our recognizing, both the perimeter, or part(s) of the perimeter, and the mass or form of the shaped area. Highlighted maps are

fascinating, because they often imply geographic relief or even separation from a horizontal plane. By removing or lifting the geographic area from its surroundings, they emphasize certain "geographic" qualities of place in that they imply that it is a part of the earth's crust that has depth or vertical mass. The most interesting maps of this type are rendered in bas-relief, or are sculpted out of their medium (such as concrete); thus the actual shadow of the map or background forms the image we see.

On occasion, one sees combinations of the three techniques, as when a silhouette map is combined with the outline map technique. These "composite" maps in effect reaffirm both the solid massing and the perimeter of the mapped area. But they add another dimension—a kind of synergism—that none of the techniques alone is capable of capturing. When a silhouette map is outlined, the mapped area possesses a type of action or implied animation in that the border is defined and yet unstable; it seems to have a kind of expansive energy because we are not exactly sure which outline defines the image.

In the hands of creative cartographers and designers, these techniques can be further manipulated to produce very exciting and interesting maps. Consider, for example, a map designer producing a map using only *part* of its outline and relying on the map reader to "add" the remaining information from memory or imagination and hence to become a participant in the cartographic process—that is, to enter the dialogue between mapmaker and map reader. At this point, it may be argued, the mapmaker ceases to be a "cartographer" and becomes a "graphic designer." However, that distinction holds only if we forget that cartographers have, for centuries, employed ingenious techniques that make maps more attractive, interesting, and intriguing—as well as simply more informative.

Cartographers also categorize maps by the perspective that mapmakers use. Most commonly seen maps of Texas are drawn from a *planimetric* perspective, that is, as if we were looking straight down at the state from a spacecraft. One also sees oblique maps, that is, those that are drawn as if we were looking toward the horizon, so that our view intersects the ground at an angle (such maps of smaller areas are called "birds-eye views"). Oblique maps remind us that maps are simply representations of places; they can be highly accurate or stylized and still qualify as maps.

In examining Texas maps, we encounter yet another kind of map—the three-dimensional solid, which may be made out of metal, glass, cement, or wood (fig. 1-2). These maps may be used for monuments, paving stones, and signs. They are created by accretion (as when cement is poured into a mold) or by excavation or subtraction (as when a Texas-shaped image is cut out of a sheet of plywood). Their thickness may permit the map to stand freely.

FIG. 1-2. These stepping stones are made of terrazzo (stone aggregate in cement) and are approximately 2' at their widest dimension and 3" thick. They are reminiscent of relief maps that have been produced by cartographers in many different materials. (1991 photo by author)

Although such three-dimensional maps may seem to break with tradition, they should remind us that early maps were often made of sticks or clay. Thus, maps have been part of both literary history and the history of material culture. To appreciate any map—including the map of Texas—we must view it in what cartographic historian Brian Harley calls "the three contexts of cartography":[1]

- Its relationship to *other maps;* that is, how is it similar to, or different from, maps of the same area.
- Its relationship to *mapmakers,* which is to say, the person or people who made the map and other people who produced similar maps.
- Its relationship to *society;* all maps are artifacts of a culture, for they tell us much about the way people view the world and their surroundings.

Maps are products of their times, and a visually oriented society like ours, which is concerned with power, trade, and influence, emphasizes geopolitical identities such as continents, countries, states, and even counties. We come to recognize familiar map shapes because they spell out our relationship to people in spatial terms. As we look at a U.S. map, for example, we see that some states, like Iowa, Wisconsin, Texas, and Idaho, are more easily recognized than others. Perhaps not coincidentally, these are states that have distinctive shapes and distinctive images.

In studying these familiar map shapes, we need to ask ourselves a fundamental question: Do we recognize them because of something intrinsically unique about their shape or form, or because we have seen them repeatedly used in promotion and advertising? Consider the map of Iowa, which has come to be associated with products and services of the Hawkeye State—such as juicy hams—or the map of Wisconsin, which has been used to promote the state's dairy products. In each case, the state map serves as a mnemonic device by which we associate a place and a commodity. Through a complex thought process, cartography and image building can support each other. A name (Idaho), a product (potatoes), and a shape (an oddly configured state with a distinctive "panhandle") can be integrated in the (public) mind. Maps, in other words, help bring narrative and visual languages together. They are part of our vocabulary.

Is there anything inherently special about certain state outlines—something that makes them jump out at us in a U.S. map? And what happens when a state map stands alone—that is, is viewed by itself? When removed from the U.S. map, some are almost unrecognizable as states. Despite their scenic beauty or other attractions, Colorado or Wyoming have shapes that are so geometric (rectangular) that little or nothing can be done to help distinguish them from each other (fig. 1-3). When removed from surrounding states, their shapes become common rectangular forms, impossible to differentiate from shapes such as sheets of paper, window frames, or rectangular traffic signs; hence their maps are very rarely used in advertising and promotion.

On the other hand, the map of Ohio is rather distinctive because of the state's sinuous Ohio River profile along its southern border and its curving Lake Erie profile at the northern border. Thus, when we see a map of Ohio used in an agency's or company's logo or trademark, we recognize it immediately—whether or not the name "Ohio" appears with it (fig. 1-4). Because of the state's geographic position and compact shape, Ohio's map lends itself very well to, and perhaps even inspired, the catchy "Ohio, the Heart of It All" slogan used by the Ohio Department of Travel and Tourism to promote the Buckeye State. The process by which maps become symbols has not been seriously studied, but a look at the most popular state maps reveals three characteristics of easily recognized and heavily used geographic shapes:

- Proportion—the shape is often as wide at its widest as it is tall, and horizontality is favored over tall shapes (such as California).
- Variety—the perimeter or outline is based on a limited variety of memorable shapes, such as curves, bends, straight lines, and intersections of lines rather than on all straight or curved lines.
- Volume—most popular state maps have a sufficient mass, or bulk, to provide a "target" in which to place information.

certified by

FIG. 1-4. The map of Ohio is distinctively shaped and is used as a logo for private companies, organizations, and some governmental agencies. (Courtesy Ohio Association of Historical Societies and Museums)

Some state maps are very distinctive (e.g., those of Idaho, Florida, and Maryland), even to the point of being quite attenuated or distorted, but they may still lend themselves to use because their overall dimensions fill a square or rectangular format. Others, like California's, are so vertical that their potential distinctiveness is overshadowed by the inherent awkwardness of the shape. The map of California is a difficult shape in which to place much information, especially the kind of horizontally placed information our word- and writing-oriented society relies on.

Shape may also reinforce stereotypes. Can the inherently unstable graphic shape of California be subconsciously associated with the popular image of California culture as odd? Can the tall, bent shape of the Golden State contribute to its image of instability—that it is liable to fall into the Pacific? Social psychologists might have an interesting assignment working with these "subliminal" images, provided they could develop methods that specifically address how visual form (or shape) relates to mental images.

Those who use maps to determine specific locations or relationships between places may question whether "map" is the correct term for such simplified shapes. Some suggest that they should be called cartograms or cartographic designs in which the form or the design of the image is less important for its geographic content than for its associative or evocative value. Yet, even the simplest of outline maps can serve very important purposes. In that sense, the type of popular cartography that includes outline and silhouette map recognition is related to the mental or cognitive mapping studied by geographers. At their most basic, geographic outlines provide a context for activity that occurs at larger and smaller scales. State map shapes form an essential part of our image of our country as a republic. Therefore, such map shapes do help orient us in a popular culture context, for they spell out perceptual relationships, as well as spatial relationships, between people and places.

Rather than being used solely to facilitate travel and mobility, which is what we might expect from traditional maps, then, these simplified maps serve two important purposes:

1. *Orientation*. They reaffirm the relative positions of the geographic unit (for we usually first see them in the context of other states, i.e., as part of the U.S. map, and continue to do so whenever we look at a map of the country). In this regard, Texas is a fundamental feature of the U.S. map. Not simply another state, Texas is a pivotal point in the symmetry of the United States; it holds up the country, as it were. As a journalist opined, "You could spin the nation like a top with Texas as the pivotal point."[2] Texas, in shape, gives strong definition to the southern and southwestern perimeter of the country. Significantly, Texas shares a border with a foreign country—Mexico—and this helps convey a sense of territory to the map outline. Subconsciously, we know that Texas does not have just any border, but the largest international border of any state. Consider the dilemma of *Thelma and Louise*, two movie "outlaws" fleeing from Arkansas (and Oklahoma) to Mexico. Map in hand, Thelma pleads with Louise to take the most logical, which is to say, direct, route to Mexico, but Louise refuses to drive through Texas because of unpleasant past experiences there. In avoiding Texas, however, an otherwise possible escape becomes an epic and convoluted journey into the netherworld of American perceptual geography. Whether one likes Texas or not, it is an essential element in defining the geography of the entire United States.

2. *Evocation*. Even the simplest map silhouette or outline can serve as a repository for a tremendous amount of information that

we already know (or will learn) about Texas. We simply add this information to the simple shape by remembering what we have heard (or seen) about the place. Much of this information is narrative, but a good deal of it is visual or graphic; that is, the map shape becomes an associative device (or cue) that triggers memories of, say, the barren (West) Texas landscape (perhaps as stereotyped in films like *Giant*) or other images of events we have been told occurred, or things that may be found within its boundaries. Children's puzzles and some place-oriented games manipulate or create topographical or topological images. At the simplest level, one is reminded of puzzle maps that depict citrus in California, copper in Arizona, cowboys in Texas. These mental images are based on a series of educational and commercial maps appearing in the classroom and home since at least the 1920s and the 1930s. In this format, the shape of the state becomes associated with a series of educational— or informational—messages.

Take for example, two very different maps of Texas, postcard images that highlight the role of maps of various kinds in conveying information. The first is a pictographic map image showing the state's major roads, communities, and scenic resources (plate 1). Despite its simplification and abstraction, it would still be considered a map by those who demand topographic or locational information, for it conveys information about geographic positions and can be used to orient the traveler.

Compare this postcard with a humorous depiction of a Texan's view of Texas in the context of the United States (plate 2). Here the state dominates the entire country—a visual technique that emphasizes the immodesty of Texans and the sprawling image of Texas as a huge place. It is the kind of map that generates what geographers call "map shock," for it "causes the reader to pause, reflect, and register a more lasting impression than with a conventional portrayal."[3] When the *New Yorker* ran a cartoon of a New Yorker's view of the country years ago (everything west of New Jersey was reduced in size and hence importance), the shocking cartoonlike cartogram was viewed as delightfully elitist and sophisticated. The Texas postcard, however, reaffirms a kind of historical myth-fact (Texas expansionism) that is associated with the mentality of Texans in the popular mind. This image is based on a fact of American geography: Texas is the largest of the lower forty-eight states, and, as everyone knows, Texans won't let the rest of the United States forget that fact.

Next, let us consider another postcard of Texas that serves to convey a subliminal visual message about Texas—which is depicted only in outline/ silhouette form (plate 3). This is a very different kind of map, because it is not meant to help us orient Texas' actual geographic space as much as it creates an instant impression of place. We immediately know that Texas is the place being featured because we have come to recognize its distinctive shape. Therefore, the map's silhouette conveys a visual message about the place even before we read the words. The pictographic, Edenic landscape within the map gains authenticity and validity simply by positioning. We *assume* that we are being given information about Texas by the placement of an image within the map—whether the landscape featured is really Texas or not.

Maps or cartograms of this type convey authority in that they use aspects of a tool that we are taught to trust—the map—to validate a visual image of place. Despite the disarmingly simple format of its design, a cartographic device like this Texas postcard is a very powerful shaper of mental images. This one, jokingly or otherwise, associates Texas with nothing less than heaven—a point that those not sympathetic to Texas would find amusing (if not disturbing) and that those enamored of the state would find reassuring, as if the concept of a place being "God's country" leads to an enhanced image. In the case of this postcard, however, the map is used to reaffirm another Texas stereotype—that of irrational pride in the state, whether anyone else believes that pride to be justified or not. The sun's rays and the Edenic landscape add another mental image, that of creation. In other words, this postcard connotes both place and action.

A closer (or more objective) look at this postcard and other Texas maps reveals that Texas qualifies—on all three design counts—as a successful popular map shape: (1) it provides a geographic outline that has the correct (roughly 1:1 horizontal to vertical) proportions; (2) its perimeter possesses a variety of shapes (but not too many) that are immediately recognized; and (3) it provides sufficient (in this case, ample) volume or space to encourage the placement of information *within* the boundaries.

A few more Texas map products will help introduce us to the theme of the map as a powerful symbolic device. One of the most interesting and educational is the crossword puzzle produced by Charley and Guy Orbison of Denton, Texas (fig. 1-5). Their uncanny use of the map as a background for Texas-based questions about people, places, and events underscores the spatial context of the puzzle. Can any other state boast of a crossword puzzle in the shape of its map outline?

And can any other state claim the number of sports teams—college and professional—associated with a map? It is here that we can see how adaptable the Texas map is as a logo. Looking, for example, at the popular logo or symbol of the Texas Rangers (fig. 1-6), which cleverly places a baseball in the map of Texas, we see how effectively Texas-shaped cartograms can be manipulated to convey additional information about place, product, and service. In the case of the Texas Rangers' logo, the baseball does not actually fit

FIG. 1-5. This crossword puzzle tests one's knowledge of Texas history, culture, geography, and trivia. (Courtesy Charley and Guy Orbison, Denton, Texas)

FIG. 1-6. A billboard looming above Interstate Highway 35W in Fort Worth features the Texas Rangers' logo, which employs two readily recognizable images in conjunction with the baseball team's name. (1992 photo by author)

completely within the map, but is permitted to break, or distort, the state boundary. This may seem like a simple deviation, but it is important, for it means that some of the map outline of Texas can actually be omitted or distorted—a theme to which we will return—and the map still be recognizable as Texas.

Texas map signs abound along the state's highways and roads. In addition to the more or less predictable use of the map on official highway designation signs (fig. 1-7), we see the Texas map quite often associated with private roadside advertising. Texas Safari provides a case in point, and drivers along highways in Central Texas are quite familiar with its signs featuring safari imagery and the Texas map (fig. 1-8). We first see the face of a wild animal (a lion), but soon realize that it is set into the map of Texas. Here, again, we see only a partial map—the lion's shaggy mane obscures the eastern border—but one that is quite recognizable as Texas. The Texas Safari signs are smaller than billboards and pack a lot of information into a design that the average

Maps and Identity ★ 21

FIG. 1-7. Texas highway signs, like those in many states, use the map to verify that the road being driven on is a state-owned or state-maintained highway. (1991 photo by author)

FIG. 1-8. Graphic imagery used in Texas Safari signs beckon the motorist by linking the exotic with the familiar and establishing a popular comparison of Africa and Texas as similarly vast and untamed. (1992 photo by author)

motorist has less than seven seconds to interpret at sixty miles per hour. The use of the map subconsciously reaffirms Texas in the naming and location of this parklike zoo, and this may help orient, and attract, out-of-state tourists to a genuine Texas attraction. The wild animal may also help reaffirm that Texas has an exotic, perhaps wild and untamed, character. In reality, the savannah-like landscape near the Texas park *does* resemble parts of Africa, especially Kenya.

To the exotic we may add the frontier or "western" character of Texas as part of the state's image and identity: Texas is historic and exotic—qualities that are reaffirmed in the creative "Republic of Texas" logo seen along San Antonio's River Walk (plate 5). The words (and image) imply that Texas is somehow separate from the rest of the United States (which it indeed was from 1836 until 1845), and the sign's red, white, and blue colors reaffirm a separate national political identity.

As we observe Texas maps, we often see the star used in association with it, either to mark the location of a business or community or simply to convey a sense of identity. The ultimate combination of map and star appears in corporate identities such as the aptly named Texas Star Roofing Company of Dallas. Texas Star's name encourages the use of both the map and the star in advertising its roofing services. The sign's red, white, and blue colors would seem to be a natural choice for a name with such underlying political connotations.

The map of Texas is even used to advertise the services and products of national (or international) companies that normally defend their identity very aggressively. Consider, for example, McDonald's fast food restaurants. They not only market a Texas Homestyle Burger in Texas, but also use the Texas map on both outdoor advertising, such as billboards, and product wrappers (fig. 1-9). In this type of advertising, we see a common design theme: an outline map in which the mass of the state serves as a background in which to place a slogan that promotes both the product and Texas. Among soft drink distributors, Pepsi-Cola appears to be the most active user of the state map; we see its trucks and soft drink cartons festooned with red, white, and blue Texas maps. This helps the bottler claim a Texas market and a Texas identity.

In a particularly effective use of the Texas map, HC International Trade, Inc., of Dallas, markets a makeup compact called "The Eyes of Texas," which is also the title of a famous Texas folk song. When opened, the Texas-shaped compact reveals two dozen labeled compartments containing makeup bearing names like Texas Crude, Adobe, Yellow Rose, Tumbleweed, Bluebonnet, and Armadillo (plate 4). These compartments remind us of counties, perhaps, and they help emphasize the geographic diversity of the Lone Star State while reminding us of other Texas stereotypes.

The map of Texas is so recognizable that we may see it substituting for the name "Texas," as in an advertisement where the silhouette forms the last "word" in a sentence: "The finest quality and selection in . . ." (fig. 1-10). This is an effective form of subliminal advertising, for consumers are affected by a subconscious message while they are participating in the advertising process by completing the sentence. We often see the map on billboards and in other graphic advertising, where it reinforces the word "Texas" in the mind of the traveler and reader. This positioning reminds us that the Texas map is closely tied to popular perceptions of the state. Used as a graphic and narrative device, it is often associated with both Texas geography and history—that is, space/place and time. Moreover, the map means Texas as both a word and a concept that refers to all things Texan. In this sense, the map helps create a sense of identity.

FIG. 1-9. A state map on a McDonald's burger wrapper lends authenticity to the product. Portions of the outline are obscured, but the map remains recognizable. (Courtesy McDonald's)

FIG. 1-10. A map silhouette substitutes for the last word in a sentence of advertisement copy. (Courtesy The Tie Market, Dallas, Texas)

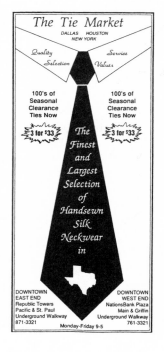

When I use the word "identity" in this context, I am referring to three concepts:

1. *Integrity.* Oneness or wholeness—that is, the sameness of essential or generic character that constitutes the reality of a thing. The map of Texas unifies a wide range of images into a single entity. In reality, we know that Texas is a very complex place that features

diverse peoples and landscapes. Texas embodies several cultural traits and varied regional characteristics, as Jordan et al. demonstrate in *Texas: A Geography*.[4] The map helps emphasize the unity of what are, in reality, disparate Texas identities.

2. *Character.* Persistence of personality—in the vernacular voice of popular psychology, we experience an "identity crisis" when we are not sure of who we are. Identity, in this sense, refers to a kind of integrity of being, which is to say, a manifestation of actual structure or composition. Texas has an image based in part on personality: stereotypically, we associate Texas with size (territory), frontier settlement, cultural traditions, and wealth; all of these components help reaffirm a persistent identity that is part fact and part fiction.

3. *Authenticity.* Condition of sameness as that being described or asserted. Under this definition, identity equals veracity. When we learn something is truly the same as that which it purports to be, or is suspected of being, we assume that the identity of the thing is confirmed. This definition further reminds us that identities authenticate the real thing. In the case of the Texas map, we may say that an abstract shape or outline is authentically Texan because there is nothing else with the same shape. The map of Texas conveys the sense of being the real thing, or the genuine article, because it fits all the criteria we demand.

As we shall see, the map of Texas is closely tied to the state's identity, which is to say, its image, personality, and integrity. That is why David Byrne used it so effectively in his 1986 film *True Stories,* a surreal and enchanting look at the lives of Texans in the fictional small town of Virgil during the 1986 Texas sesquicentennial.[5] Byrne's film begins with a personal history of Texas followed by images of a dozen Texas maps featuring chilies, marbles, denim, leather, and the Alamo; these maps help link the place or location with the lives of the film's characters. The maps themselves help convey a sense of Texas identity. In Byrne's film, Virgil, Texas, seems to epitomize the state as embodied in a nearly mystical landscape and Anglo/Hispanic/African American population.

Few events generate (and confirm) a sense of identity more than do football games, and the University of Texas at Austin marching band epitomizes the use of the map—usually at the beginning of the UT-Oklahoma game—by forming a huge human map of the state on the football field (fig. 1-11). By so doing, the band not only proves its Texas identity, it subtly stakes out the "turf" as Texas property.

This theme, Texas as a territory as well as a place, is quite common. Part of the identity of Texans is expansiveness, and the map reminds us that Texas is both space and place.

FIG. 1-11. A human map of Texas is formed by the University of Texas at Austin marching band before the start of the school's annual football game with the University of Oklahoma. This formation exemplifies the concept of loyalty to place. (1994 photo courtesy Maurice Wilson, Austin, Texas)

FIG. 1-12. Until 1994, a silhouette of the Texas map was creatively integrated in a Dallas radio station's lettering. (Courtesy radio station KRLD)

In proclaiming a geographic identity, a map need not be large; in fact, some of the most interesting and effective Texas maps are small accents in larger visual designs. A fascinating variant of the silhouette map is seen in the initials of Dallas-based News Radio Station KRLD, which confirms its Texas identity by manipulating the open space in the letter R into a Texas map (fig. 1-12). The radio station used this almost subliminal map in its logo and promotional material, including bumper stickers. Similarly, the Southwest Conference uses the Texas map by subtraction; in its logo, the form (silhouette) of Texas is excavated from the letter "C," a subliminal reminder that Texas, and the universities in the conference, is part of the region. The Texas map has also been used as empty space between initials in other advertising, for example, between the T and the A in the Texas Avionics and Texas Aviation Services logo.

One can convey a sense of Texas by using empty space in a graphic, but the map also makes a very effective three-dimensional design. Perhaps the most stunning artifactual Texas maps are those produced at the University of Texas at Arlington's Automation and Robotics Research Institute (fig. 1-13). Visitors from all over the world are given demonstrations of the high-quality three-dimensional images that can be cut out of glass (and even

FIG. 1-13. Cut out of plate glass at the Automation and Robotics Research Institute at the University of Texas at Arlington, this small, three-dimensional souvenir reminds visitors of the relationship between Texas and the high-tech industry. (Author's collection)

metal) by robotically controlled high-pressure hoses that propel water and finely ground aggregate at fifty thousand pounds per square inch. These, we might say, are the ultimate composite map shapes, for they are three-dimensional silhouettes. According to project director John Mills, of all the shapes that could have been used, the map of Texas was the most natural for reaffirming the project's identity with Texas.[6] Among the most sophisticated of souvenirs, these maps are brought home by visitors from other states and foreign countries as reminders of Texas' special place in high-tech industry. These maps are truly iconic in that they come to symbolize Texas to the individual who possesses—or experiences—them.

Although image and identity are highly personal, they are also public in that they are shared. This explains why the Texas map makes such a good political symbol. Consider, for example, the image of Texas in the 1992 presidential race, which found all three candidates—incumbent George Bush, independent contender Ross Perot, and Democratic nominee Bill Clinton—claiming Texas roots. Whereas Perot could claim Texas nativity and Clinton early Texas family roots, Bush was negatively portrayed by critics as someone whose only claim to residency consisted of a hotel suite in Houston. Bush scurried to maintain his native-son status by making at least a dozen visits to Texas, seven in the last weeks of the campaign. Bush bumper stickers bearing a map of Texas proliferated as the campaign intensified. Among the most newsworthy items of the campaign was President Bush's support of a number of Texas-based space-age industries, including the Superconducting Super Collider (SSC) in Waxahachie. For Texans, one of the most memorable campaign images was President Bush standing in front of the SSC's huge logo map of Texas (fig. 1-14). This image, a Texan supporting space-age Texas, reaffirmed the identity of George Bush and the validity of Texas' claim to the high-tech industries of the future. Although George Bush lost the election, he won Texas—perhaps as a result of his Herculean efforts to

FIG. 1-14. Determined to reaffirm his Texas ties during the 1992 presidential campaign, George Bush stands in front of the logo for the Superconducting Super Collider (SSC), a huge Texas map symbolizing the state's commitment to high technology. Both President Bush and the SSC were popular in Texas—and defeated nationally. (Courtesy SSC)

FIG. 1-15. A 1992 campaign sign for Geneva Finstad near Glen Rose, Texas, reveals seventeen Texas maps. (Photo by author)

link his own image and identity with that of his adopted state.

At all levels, candidates in Texas believe that they benefit from association with the state. Thus, during the 1992 campaign for the Texas legislature we saw roadside signs for candidates—some of whom used the Texas map. Among the most interesting were those of Democrat Geneva Finstad, whose signs bore not only a bright red Texas map showing the candidate's home district, but also sixteen white silhouette maps in a diamond-shaped blue border (fig. 1-15). Although Finstad lost the election, her campaign signs reveal how the Texas map is used by designers: it may serve as the centerpiece or be an accent subliminally repeated for effect. Although the use of the Texas map does not ensure success of a candidate or a product, many advertisers and strategists use it in the hope that it will.

In this chapter the groundwork has been laid for us to look more closely, and critically, at the map of Texas as a symbol of state and regional identity. In the chapters that follow, we shall examine the map of Texas as few maps have ever been studied, namely, as an emerging popular art form. More than one hundred Texas maps will be described or illustrated. By analyzing their form in relation to the other graphic and visual information associated with them, we will see that even the smallest and simplest of Texas maps can be charged with significant historical and geographical content and meaning.

2.
The Shape of Texas

Just look at your average map of the United States. What's the first thing you
notice? Texas.

—Thom Marshall,
"Stately Shape Y'all Know"

THE MAP OF TEXAS IS USED TO ADVERTISE AND PROMOTE PRODUCTS AND SERVICES
in both the private and the public sectors. One consequence of the map's
intense promotion is, naturally, high visibility and instant recognition. No
state map is used more aggressively or effectively than the map of Texas, and
no state map is more readily recognized by the public. The Computer Support Corporation of Dallas creatively incorporates it into the cover of its
popular *Arts and Letters Clip Art Handbook for Computers* (1990), on which
we see the state's outline amid many other recognizable shapes such as scis-
sors, a soda pop bottle, and a dove (plate 6). Even though this map of Texas
is not perfectly accurate, it reinforces the image of Texas as a geographic
entity and an interesting shape. As part of its geographic, or spatial, graphics, this software program provides a sample map on which to locate places;
this map, as might be guessed, is of Texas. It is also significant that England-
based PC Globe, Inc., chose to use a map of Texas to illustrate its map and
utilities functions in an advertisement in the November, 1991, issue of *Geographical* magazine. Texas, in the popular mind, has come to symbolize both
space and place.

Those who study popular culture might assume that the map of Texas is
recognized so readily simply because it is so heavily used, that is, because we
have been "conditioned" into recognizing it because it is seen so often. This,
coupled with the facts that Texans are proud of their state and think spa-
tially (i.e., they conceive of Texas as a large place that has important boundaries), goes a long way toward explaining the popularity of the map as icon
or symbol.

The more we study the map of Texas, however, the more we become aware
that other, more purely design-related, factors are at work. When discussing

the map of Texas, many people volunteer information about the map image itself and how it draws their attention; therefore, we need to carefully consider the inherent shape of the Texas outline—that is, what it is about the intrinsic design qualities of the map image that may initially encourage its use. Taking a good look at the map of Texas as an abstract image, we see that it has important design characteristics that are possessed by no other state map.

Let us begin by studying the map as an abstract form capable of evoking thoughts or emotions in the manner of the Rorschach tests that psychologists employ. What messages does the map of Texas convey as a shape or form? Looked at in this way, the state's outline is quite associative; that is, it brings certain abstract images to mind. Subconsciously, the Texas map outline seems to be viewed as a utilitarian shape. Many respondents mention that, like a tool, perhaps a knife or a dagger, it has a "handle" (the Panhandle) at the "top" and a (curving) tip or point at the "bottom." One respondent told me that it reminds her of two other Texas icons—a boot topped by a cowboy hat, or, as she described it, the "lower [southern] half is like a boot, while the Panhandle's square top reminds me of a ten-gallon hat." One does see cartoonlike map images of Texas with a cowboy hat atop the Panhandle—perhaps a literal (or very graphic) interpretation of the respondent's image. The map and cowboy imagery have been linked, as in the case of a popular 1930s political cartoon by Parrish, which depicted Vice-President John Nance Garner riding a rearing horse, the saddle of which was in the shape of Texas; the Panhandle was the saddle horn and the southern tip, the stirrups.

There is also a darker, or at least a more Freudian, image associated with the map of Texas. A few (mostly non-Texan) respondents have noted that the map of Texas has a sexual connotation; that is, they describe it in reference to male (genital) anatomy. Some people do read either the Panhandle or southern tip, or both, as phallic in form—possibly in association with Texas' aggressive "cowboy" image. These people, and their unflattering analogy, are presumably in the minority. After all, if the shape were *too* evocative or "explicit" it probably would lose its value as an icon that can substitute for Texas the place. These people may be projecting pejorative or negative images onto the map as it signifies the stereotypical crudeness of Texans. Such associative meanings are deeply personal and have their limitations. If anything, the map of Texas means many things to many people as a literal symbol. It is the *ambiguity* of the shape of Texas that ensures its symbolic use.

The unusual shape of Texas is reaffirmed by how rarely one sees anything natural, such as rocks or glass shards, shaped like it. Few natural objects would contain the combination of curves and angles that make up the map, but I am reminded that one Texan proudly displays a cross section of petrified wood with a roughly Texas-shaped outline. This was a real find. So, too, was a roughly Texas-shaped automobile water pump cross section that so reminded its owner (and all who saw it) of Texas that he framed it and used it as both art and a conversation piece. Normally, however, most shapes look nothing like the Texas map, and one would have to consciously cut and saw a shape into a Texas map with considerable care for it to pass as a map. Put simply, the shape of Texas is unlikely to occur naturally or accidentally. That is why Bevo, a longhorn steer with a natural Texas-shaped marking on his forehead, drew such attention at stock shows (and from the media) in the 1980s. And it also explains why a filly emblazoned with a reverse image of Texas on her right flank (fig. 2-1) was featured in an illustrated newspaper article titled "Horse of a Different Color."[1] The horse was originally named Gypsy by her owner, Mary Harbit Hecox of West Columbia, Texas, but neighbors insist on calling the horse by its more obvious nickname, Miss Texas.[2]

In terms of its design dynamics, the primary synergistic thrust of Texas is both outward and downward. Because the state tapers to a point, some see it as an inherently unstable shape that can tip over, or at least "wobble." Postmodern art critic Dave Hickey has noted of Texas' outline: "It's very unstable" in the way it appears to stand on its bent southern extreme.[3] A very evocative use of the map finds it transformed into a tornado on the cover of George Bomar's book on Texas weather (fig. 2-2); this, of course, is the ultimate "Texas twister."

Considered morphologically, that is, aside from any associative aspects such as tornadoes, boots, and cowboy hats, the map of Texas is highly distinctive. No other state possesses such a combination of points, curves, and rectangles, which prompts a critic of design to comment that Texas has "three distinct kinds of borders. There are three wavy parabolic river borders. Then it's got five Euclidian geometric borders. And then this long crinkly border you would call a fractal line that is the Gulf Coast."[4]

The combination of shapes in the Texas map makes for instantaneous distinction from other states—an essential requirement for something that serves as a symbol or icon. Nevertheless, portions of the Texas map may be confused with other places (continents and countries rather than other states), which is to say that the Texas map is also stereotypically "geographical." That may help to explain why it is sometimes used synonymously with "place" or "territory."

As a cartographic representation, the outline of Texas is somewhat evocative of the larger land masses on the world map. With its bulging central section and its distorted, triangular base, the abstract proportions of Texas are eminently continental, perhaps basically subcontinental in shape, vaguely reminding us of South America, Africa, or, especially, the Indian subcontinent (fig. 2-3). Significantly, while I was completing these comparison maps of Texas and India, a student asked why I had drawn a Texas map with a small piece missing from the Panhandle.

FIG. 2-1. Nicknamed Miss Texas by the locals, this filly owned by Mary Harbit Hecox of West Columbia, Texas, has a spot in the shape of a Texas map's reverse image. (Courtesy Mary Harbit Hecox)

FIG. 2-2. The cover of George Bomar's *Texas Weather* makes evocative use of the state map. (Courtesy University of Texas Press, Austin, Texas)

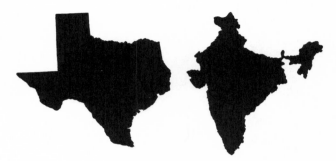

FIG. 2-3. Silhouette maps of Texas and India placed side by side show that Texas has a distinctive (sub)continental shape. In this comparison, India has been *reduced* by approximately 50 percent. (Maps by author)

Although the shape or outline of Texas helps confirm the state's size, uniqueness, and geographic position and in so doing helps brand Texans as a unique people, its carrot-shaped outline may explain why it is so effectively used to market exotic products, as we saw in its use in the Texas Safari advertising. Subliminally, perhaps, Texas also reminds us of Africa in that it is southern, isolated, and exotic.

The geographic concepts we associate with Texas—a sprawling state that stretches almost half a continent in width—help color our views of the shape of the state. Ask people about the proportions of Texas, for example, and many will say it is much wider than it is tall. Texas seems to stretch interminably east and west, but in terms of its basic design, the map fits almost perfectly into a circle or a square (fig. 2-4). Those who have survived the fourteen-hour drive across the state would be sobered to learn that driving from the tip to the Panhandle to the border with Mexico is even more excruciating, requiring nearly twenty hours. Proportionately, we think Texas is much wider than it is and underestimate its height as a graphic. That makes us think of Texas as more horizontal (wider) than vertical, but it isn't—at least not by much: the state is 97 percent as tall as it is wide.

The Texas map outline, in other words, fills a cubic frame. That basic fact of geometry often leads to the Texas map's being set in a circular or square design format, as it is in the seal of the Texas Historical Commission (fig. 2-5). When the map is nestled into a circle, the graphic has the effect of containing the expansive outline of the state in a "global" setting. With humor, *Texas Monthly* used this graphic effect on the cover of its February, 1993, issue, which featured an artist's satellite view of an Earth with only one huge continent in the shape of Texas.

Considering that most maps are printed on rectangular sheets of paper, we can understand that some commercial mapmakers separate the Pan-

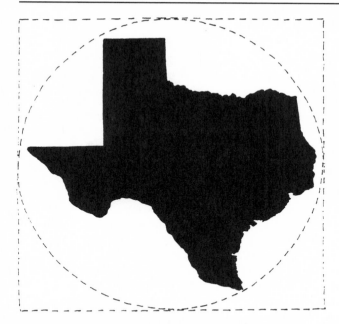

FIG. 2-4. Neatly fitting into a circle and a square, the shape of Texas is as tall as it is wide, a design feature that encourages its use as a self-contained graphic device. (Graphic by author)

FIG. 2-5. On historical markers, the Texas Historical Commission uses the map in a circular format. Called the medallion, the circumscribed map is in effect an official seal that emphasizes the partial symmetry of the state's outline. (Photo by author)

handle and sometimes the southern tip (with the notation "see reverse side," or "see inset" for the Panhandle) from the rest of the state. Lest we think that this breaking up of the image is a modern phenomenon of road maps, we should note that it has been practiced by cartographers since 1852. Some relatively popular maps—including school atlas maps—used the technique in part to depict the more populous eastern portion of the state in more detail, that is, at a larger scale. The Texas Department of Transportation in 1993 stopped the practice of separating the Panhandle from the rest of the state, thus ending motorists' search on the map for Amarillo in Central New Mexico![5]

This reminds us of a basic fact of Texas geography: since the state's inception, there has been a discrepancy between territory (i.e., land area) and population distribution. The significant communities are located in a triangle in East and Northeast Texas and have been since the middle to late nineteenth century.

Squinting at a map of Texas makes us more aware of another important aspect of its morphology, namely, its dynamism or inherent energy. Texas is, without question, our most "expansive" state in shape or outline—a distorted cross consisting of vertical and horizontal elements that intersect at a point somewhat off center. When viewed abstractly, the image of Texas is roughly cruciform, a combination of points (south and west) and blocks (north and east) protruding from a solid mass. San Antonio's Texas Med-Clinic makes good use of Texas as a cross, which also symbolizes health services (fig. 2-6). The map can be twisted into a "t," as in the very interesting logo of the Texas Iron and Metal Company of Houston (fig. 2-7). This may be the ultimate in the subliminal relationship between a map as graphic device and as narrative device, for it reaffirms the first letter in the state's name.

When distorted into a cross, the power of the Texas map as a graphic device is obvious: the two powerful rectangular masses forming Texas intersect at a point slightly off center and create a sense of visual tension. In one sense, this divergence of axes creates an inherently powerful visual vaguely reminiscent of the swastika (which, before its appropriation by the Nazis, was a popular symbol in many cultures in both the Old and the New Worlds).

And yet, if we equate the shape of Texas with any form, it is the five- (possibly six-) pointed star. In fact, more respondents associate the map with a star than any other single shape. Interestingly, a number of informants describing Texas logos could not remember if the image of Texas they had seen was a map or a star. This may help account for the fact that many people believe that the map has been used for a very long time to connote Texas. No other state map has such an array of points or protuberances that protrude from a central massing, which is to say that, although Texas is not shaped like a perfect star, it is more star-shaped than any other state.

Texas MedClinic

777 N. E. Loop 410, San Antonio, Texas 78209

FIG. 2-6. San Antonio's Texas MedClinic logo renders Texas in the shape of a cross—a technique that makes use of the Texas map's roughly cruciform nature. (Courtesy Texas MedClinic, San Antonio)

FIG. 2-7. Another version of the map of Texas as cruciform, a 1992 advertisement for Texas Iron and Metal Company of Houston reminds us that the word Texas begins with a "t." (Reproduced with permission of Southwestern Bell Yellow Pages, Inc.; all rights reserved)

FIG. 2-8. This Humble Oil company car decal from the early 1950s employs a circular/star-shaped design format—a cartographer's compass rose—reminding us that Texas has an expansive, vaguely stellar shape. (Author's collection)

One often sees the Texas map and the (lone) star combined to form a very powerful graphic design. The integration of the map and the star is seen in a 1950s-era Humble Oil decal (fig. 2-8). This intriguing design uses a compass rose to validate Texas as territory, for that cartographic device is often seen

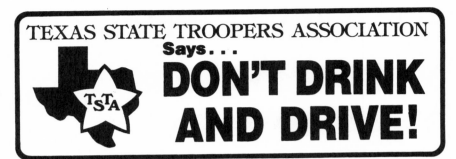

FIG. 2-9. The Texas State Troopers Association makes effective use of the star and the Texas map in this 1992 bumper sticker. (Photo by author)

FIG. 2-10. The Texas Steel Culvert Company logo features a star with the Texas map filling four of the five points. (Photo by author)

on world maps or on maps of very large geographic areas. Throughout the state, one sees many examples of the map's being combined with, or transformed into, a star. The Texas State Trooper's Association (fig. 2-9), the Texas Steel Culvert Company (fig. 2-10), and many businesses using the words "Lone Star" in their name use the map's inherently stellar shape to design advantage. Significantly, the most acute or sharpest elements of the Texas outline are those at the south and west of the image—a visual thrust that may (subconsciously) confirm both the "southern" and the "southwestern" position of the state in the overall Sunbelt-oriented perceptual geography of the nation. That, as we have seen, relates to the inherently unstable southern (lower) portion of the Texas map's shape.

Although the roughly cruciform or stellar outline of Texas fits into either a square or a circular outline, it is not symmetrical. Internally, one finds a large block of space in what is coincidentally the most populous part of the state: south central and northeast Texas. This "bulge" invites the placement of visual information *inside* the outline that reaffirms Texas ownership or affiliation or validates a product or service placed within it. Some of the

FIG. 2-11. BIZMART office products "Super Centers" are given a Texas identity through a 1992 graphic in the same genre as the "Texas-Made" or "Made by Texans" slogans that often appear in the map. (Reproduced with permission of Southwestern Bell Yellow Pages, Inc.; all rights reserved)

more commonly seen Texas maps contain the words "Texas-Made," "Made in Texas," or "Made by Texans" inside their perimeter. An advertisement for Bizmart Super Centers is typical, for it features the words "Texas Based, Texas Proud" in a slogan that crosses much of the state (fig. 2-11).

That Bizmart ad illustrates another common Texas map technique: the map is not a simple outline but is rendered as a solid form with a well-defined, shadowed edge typical of relief maps. One informant said that this edge reminded him of a "cookie cutter outline." As we have seen, this relief or shadowing technique helps give an impression of solidity and perhaps verifies that Texas is *land* (or earth) rather than simply space on a map.

Many businesses use the Texas map to pinpoint their actual locations (most often with a star) within the state's borders. This, too, helps make the map less abstract and more utilitarian. The location of a business being so indicated also validates the products or services as "Texan"; that is, it confirms the validity of the business as actually initiated by, and employing and serving, Texans. Dallas-based Minyard's grocery stores use a star inside the map silhouette to indicate their location (fig. 2-12). By adding a slogan, "since 1932," they also affirm the stability of the business. When Texas-shaped maps illustrate the location of something, such as a business or city, they help fix observers in a specific place within a huge geographic area that they are likely to have seen very little of; in other words, they authenticate existence in a huge geographic area called Texas.

Looking at the map of Texas as a graphic designer might, we see that it embodies two seemingly opposing design forces: centrifugal, whereby the form encourages us to look at, or beyond, the edges or boundaries; and centripetal, wherein our attention is focused to the inside of the form as our eye is drawn inward toward the center. Thus, the perimeter of Texas makes an exciting, contradictory graphic in that it simultaneously encourages us to look toward the core (reminding one that anything placed within it is undeniably Texan) and also toward the periphery. "Deep in the Heart of Texas" refers to a state of mind as well as to a vaguely mythical place safely situated

FIG. 2-12. In poster advertisements such as the one seen here in the window of their Arlington store, Dallas-based Minyard's grocery stores effectively use the map to convey a sense of tradition, continuity, and place. (1991 photo by author)

well within the rambling borders of the state. The map of Texas defends or shelters a way of life by emphasizing a central nucleus. Graphically, the heart—like the center of a starfish or the converging axes of a cross—is the focus of centripetal energy. A billboard for Inner Space Caverns near Georgetown, Texas, uses a map with a brightly colored heart marking the location of the caverns; the attraction's slogan, "deep in the heart of Texas," is a play on words and a reference to a nearly sacred place in Texas thought. This again confirms that maps embody both pictures (graphic imagery) and words (narrative language).

There is no better way to advertise a Texas product or service than to place a picture of it, or words about it, within the map boundaries. Small wonder, then, that many companies use the map both to identify what they sell and to mark the location of their business enterprises. One sees an incredible array of objects and products, such as automobiles, houses, trees, and foods, located in the map. Furthermore, some advertisers nearly fill the map with wording or sales pitches, such as an advertisement for dentures that uses a silhouette map as a background or the admonition of the Texas secretary of state to vote (fig. 2-13).

As might be expected, the map of Texas is often used by companies that have the word "Texas" in their names. Moreover, the map appears to be a good place to exhibit a slogan about the product or service marketed: 61 percent of the maps in a survey of the Texas Yellow Pages did so.[6] Television

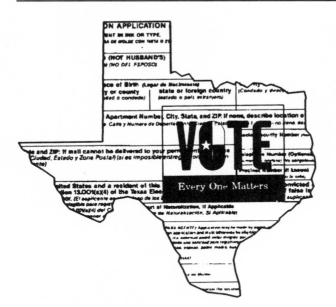

FIG. 2-13. A map was used to deliver a civic-minded message as part of a 1992 voter registration drive in Texas. (Author's collection)

ads that ran in 1992 for "Your North Texas Geo Dealers" used the map effectively. The familiar Chevrolet logo was placed inside the map, as were two Geo automobiles. Significantly, the Chevrolet symbol is a very powerful horizontal graphic that reaffirms the east-west expanse of Texas. One sees Chevrolet cars and pickup trucks with a familiar advertising slogan "Heartbeat" emblazoned across Texas outline maps affixed to the vehicles (fig. 2-14). Significantly, this slogan began as "the Heartbeat of America" in the 1970s, but in Texas the state replaces the nation as context. We see similar decals on Ford trucks and vehicles with the tongue-in-cheek slogan "The Hoofbeat." Certainly, "hoofbeat" conveys more of the sense of Texas action—and machismo associated with ranching—than "heartbeat" does.

In studying Texas map advertising for style and content, one is impressed with how often the map is used to convey a kind of action and power as opposed to stability or stasis. If the map were analyzed as a linguistic device, we might say that it can serve as both a noun (substituting for Texas as the name of a place) and a verb or perhaps adverb (Texas, the place in which something happens). This should remind us that it is literally impossible to separate the unique five-letter word "Texas" from its map. As geographer Yi Fu Tuan has noted, "Speech is a component of the total force that transforms nature into a human place."[7] The word "Texas" has become synonymous not only with a distinctive shape, but also with energy and action; Texas not only is, but things also happen in, and to, it. The map is a perfect stage on which verbal and graphic actions interact. Consider, for example,

FIG. 2-14. A familiar automobile decal in the Lone Star State, the combination of the Texas map and the Chevrolet design logo and slogan create a regional identity for a product. (Photo by author)

the FDIC's intriguing advertisement that urges the reader to "Lasso Some Land in Texas" (fig. 2-15). The map, which is shadowed to remind the prospective buyer that it is land (or, in this case, real estate) that is being offered, is actually being lassoed—a play on pictures that conveys images of ranching via the metaphor of lassoing cattle. This ingenious ad brings action, enterprise, the Wild West, and other images together. So, of course, does the concept "Texas" in the public mind.

Because the shape or outline of the Texas map is also centrifugal (or radiant), it has naturally come to symbolize expansion, or expansiveness. As Texas has become the second most populous state in the United States, the map serves well as a territorial symbol of growth. The map of Texas, then, is associated with both a specific geographic location (stability) as well as change and growth (instability). In a particularly effective use of the map to convey the changing quantity of water that will be needed to sustain Texas' population in the next half century (to 2040), the Arlington Water Utilities uses a vignette containing five overlapping outline maps that preserve the basic shape of Texas while conveying a sense of expansion (fig. 2-16). This technique perpetuates the association between Texas, geographic expansionism, and growth while it shows that a map can make an effective graph as well as an effective graphic device.

The now familiar logo of Texas Instruments (TI), first introduced in the early 1950s, provides a good example of the shape of Texas as a framework for action. The letters seem to push out the top of the map (fig. 2-17). This design reaffirms the company's identity, its Texas origins, and, very importantly, the expansiveness of the company and the state. In doing so, it relies on a common technique in popular Texas mapping: the placement of other graphic designs or text to partially obscure the map outline. This technique confirms a kind of dynamism we associate with Texas and Texans. In many

LASSO SOME LAND IN TEXAS

FIG. 2-15. In this clever 1992 FDIC advertisement in Dallas–Fort Worth area newspapers and flyers, the images convey a sense of territory, ownership, and action. (Author's collection)

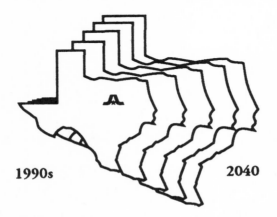

FIG. 2-16. An effective use of outline maps by the City of Arlington Water Utilities department in 1992 signifies growth and the projected increase in water consumption. (Author's collection)

1990s   2040

Water conservation is for <u>all</u> of us

Texas map graphics, objects and words virtually burst from the map. One of the more exciting graphics of this kind is seen in the logo for the 1991 Greater Southwest Guitar Show in Dallas and Austin, wherein the neck of an electric guitar protrudes eastward from the body of the state (fig. 2-18). One actually does see electric guitars in the shape of Texas, so the logo is based on fact as well as imagination.

More subdued, perhaps, are maps that more or less conform to the real outline. The Texas Hot Dog Company at the Parks Mall in Arlington uses two types of maps to convey a Texas identity. Its sign above the shop in the Mall's food court uses a subtle embossed, rather accurately shaped, alumi-

FIG. 2-17. The familiar Texas Instruments logo was first developed in 1952 and appears to be the first international use of the Texas map in advertising and promotion. (Reprinted by permission of Texas Instruments)

FIG. 2-18. The logo for the 1991 Greater Southwest Guitar Shows in Austin and Dallas illustrates the close association between Texas and music. It also uses a familiar theme: the horizontal expansion of Texas imagery through powerful supplemental graphics—in this case, the neck of an electric guitar. (Author's collection)

num bas-relief silhouette of the Texas map (plate 7). The same enterprise boasts a somewhat distorted Texas map rendered in bright red and cream-colored tiles on the back counter of the shop. Significantly, only one of these tiles is a mirror—the location of Arlington (fig. 2-19). Though nothing more than several dozen tiles, this map serves to remind us of the business's Texas identity and reaffirms our position in the real world when we view it.

The Texas map relentlessly markets a Texas image, but the variety of maps seems almost endless. In a truly ingenious packaging technique, the simulated leather cases of Texas Instruments products often bear an embossed TI/Texas map logo, reminding us, perhaps, of the mark left by a cattle brand. A February 1992 color advertisement in the *Dallas Morning News* for auto dealer David McDavid carries the branding theme a step farther: it features a blazing branding iron with the dealership's name backed by the map of Texas (plate 8). These maps are subtle reminders of Texas as a western state.

Texas maps are used to advertise a wide range of products and services, but two in particular—home improvement and automobile repair and sales—accounted for fully 35 percent of the Texas maps used in advertising in 1991–92: home improvement, 22 percent; auto repair and sales, 13 percent; recreation, 6 percent; communication, 6 percent; health and medical, 5.5 percent; heating and air conditioning, 3.5 percent; all other, 44 percent. In the early 1980s, the distribution was slightly different: home improvement, 23 percent; financial services, 11 percent; auto repair and sales, 7 percent; recreation, 6 percent; health and medical, 6 percent; computer sales, 5.8 percent; all other, 41.2 percent.

Significantly, two of the items so dear to Texans—their cars and their homes—are well represented in Texas maps. These possessions symbolize mobility and property. Also significant, financial services were far less common in the 1991–92 survey, a manifestation of the prolonged recession that hit Texas harder and earlier than most of the rest of the country. Most significant of all, perhaps, is the observation that religion very rarely uses the Texas map; after all, most religions have readily identifiable symbols of their own, such as the cross or the star, that are readily identified and zealously protected from corruption. One most interesting exception (fig. 2-20) finds a map placed over a cross; this juxtaposition emphasizes both the Christian orientation and the Texas location of Austin's Westgate Apostolic Church.

Texas maps appear in many places—as logos on T-shirts and caps for a wide range of products, services, and organizations; as billboards; to advertise a wide range of products in the Yellow Pages; and as labels on functional products (such as big, tall, strong plastic trash bags)—where a tough "Texas" identity is desirable (fig. 2-21). Texas maps are used to market products nationally and internationally, but we should not discount their local appeal. In October, 1992, a woman at Goliad, Texas, who was selling handmade pot holders in the shape of Texas, remarked that most of her sales were local; Texans love their map as much as, and perhaps more than, tourists do.

Most tourists are aware of a profusion of Texas map souvenirs, such as sunglasses and shot glasses. Sam Wisialowski, owner of Y'alls, a chain of eight Houston stores that sell Texana, carries about four hundred items in the shape of Texas. Wisialowski confirms that much Tex-map kitsch is purchased by and for Texans, not outsiders. The average Texas kitchen may have Texas-shaped ice-cube trays, cutting boards, and cookie cutters. Lone Star Pasta is one of the more popular Texas-shaped food products, and comes attractively packaged in a transparent red, white, and blue bag that reveals thousands of Texas-shaped noodles (plate 9). Texans who are into maps may bake a cake or cookies in a Texas-shaped baking pan and pull the pan out of

FIG. 2-19. A wall mosaic behind the counter at the Texas Hot Dog Company serves as an abstract map of Texas; the general location of the enterprise is depicted using a mirror. (1992 photo by author)

FIG. 2-20. The appearance of the Texas map in religious advertisements, as in this logo used by the former Westgate Apostolic Church in Austin, is quite rare, perhaps because religions have ample and readily recognizable symbols. (Author's collection)

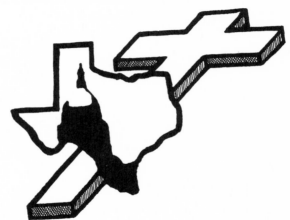

FIG. 2-21. A label for large recyclable plastic trash bags, marketed by a South Carolina company, uses the Texas map to inform customers that the bags are made from Texas raw materials. (1992 photo by author)

the oven with a Texas-shaped pot holder (fig. 2-22). Although their shapes may vary considerably, we instantly recognize these images as Texas because of the state's distinctive morphology.

From a distance, or at a quick glimpse, the map of Texas may be confused with a star or a cross. A closer look at Texas license plates (fig. 2-23) reminds us that the map and the star are sometimes interchangeable. Whereas the star had been used to separate the two groupings of letters and numbers on Texas license plates, today the map provides this type of punctuation. In the case of Texas, the *Houston Chronicle*'s placement of three small black Texas-shaped marks separating paragraphs about Texas history subtly substantiates the authenticity of "Texas Trails and Tales" articles.

In this context, Texas was one of at least nine states (along with Michigan, Minnesota, Montana, North Carolina, New Jersey, Florida, Ohio, and West Virginia) to use its map on license plates in recent years; significantly, all the states that do so meet the design criteria outlined earlier—proportions, variety, volume—that enable the map to serve as the official promotional cartograms that are seen hundreds, even thousands, of times daily. They become almost subliminal messages in that we hardly notice them at all and yet they reinforce the image of the state as a map outline.

The map, of course, takes on a connotative power or value as it is associated with the place and its products and services in the public mind. Increasingly, for example, a wide range of exported products (including groceries such as Texas okra, Texas beers, Tex-Mex foods, and Texas-style beans) have been actively marketed using the Texas map. These maps vary in their accuracy (fig. 2-24). Some are very accurate in that they bear the correct proportions and perimeter details; others are quite abstract and often involve a simplification of the perimeter. Nevertheless, they are easily identified as Texas maps. The association between map and name helps validate the products as Texan. It may also reinforce the popular image of Texas as a colorful, vaguely ethnic, and somewhat trendy part of a much larger perceptual region—the Sunbelt—where exotic or interesting products are produced, consumed, and marketed for distribution elsewhere, and where wild things happen (or happened). In this regard, we can view the logo of the show *The Best Little Whorehouse in Texas* (fig. 2-25), in which a woman's scantily clad legs protrude from the map, as the ultimate in Texas maps conveying action, though the legs on a podiatrist's map logo (fig. 2-26) are in close competition.

When a map actually *becomes* a caricature of a person through the addition of recognizable body parts or features, it can be said to be anthropomorphic. Consider, for example, two maps that acquire "personality" through human attributes. A postcard map image (plate 10) finds the map transformed into a cartoonlike caricature whose legs and arms flail as it runs with luggage in hand, while a more restful pose is provided (fig. 2-27) by a yawning

FIG. 2-22. Texas shaped pot holders, such as this one made by a Goliad resident, are especially popular and are often quilted using gingham material. (Author's collection)

FIG. 2-23. The red silhouette appearing on Texas license plates perhaps has been the most frequently seen map of Texas since 1986, when it replaced the Lone Star. (Photo by author)

FIG. 2-24. Texas food products frequently feature the map of the state. This jar of Talko' Texas pickled okra proves that a Texas map does not have to be perfectly accurate for it to be easily recognized. The relative distortion of the map conveys a lively, whimsical, almost cartoon-like quality as it effectively markets the product as authentically Texan. (Photo by author)

Texas-shaped figure that sets the mood for a San Antonio Yellow Pages advertisement for the Texas Mattress Company. Both of these images remind us that the shape of Texas is evocative and interesting enough to be manipulated into characters with personality. These are humorous examples that remind us that there is a lighter side to the use of the Texas map as well as the "straight" message that is conveyed by traditionally shaped map images. Readers interested in cartoonlike maps of Texas should consult Dennis Reinhartz for examples.[8]

Among the most interesting of Texas maps are those that are not used in advertising or for official purposes, but rather as vernacular or folk symbols on a wide range of items, from mailboxes to house addresses to clothing. We see Texas quilts and clothing embroidered with the Texas map. Among the most poignant of these Texas-shaped images are those that appear on the AIDS memorial quilt where, as Richard Meyer notes, they "figure in the decorative symbolism of individual panels" (plate 11).[9] Outdoors one sees planters in the shape of Texas. One, constructed out of logs, marks the base of a tree on a front lawn in Corsicana (fig. 2-28). Metal Texas-shaped boot scrapers are seen in front of certain businesses in the smaller towns, and we see wrought iron dinner bells in the shape of the state on occasion.

These may qualify as folk art, but some very sophisticated artistic images embodying the map are also found; the beautiful cut crystal bottles and glasses by Wilhelm Reitnauer of Fort Worth are an example (plate 12). A close look at the bridle and bit reveals a Texas-shaped map image as a crucial, if subtle, part of the sculptural form. Students of the arts would find many examples of maps in a wide variety of handmade objects; they serve as proof that the Texas map is strongly associated with all aspects of Texas culture, folk as well as elite. They also remind us that the map shape of Texas can be widely portrayed and interpreted, yet read as a map possessing the significant design features of Texas. Most, but not all, depict the four major elements of the map—the southern tip, the western point, the northern panhandle, and the northeastern bulge.

No discussion of Texas-shaped images would be complete without reference to size. Naturally, Texas maps range in size, depending on their intended use as jewelry, billboards, or earthworks, for example. The smallest Texas outline appears to be the punctuation symbol or dingbat used to end articles in *Texas Monthly* magazine: it measures about 1/8 inch on a side. Other miniature Texas maps include a small pin for an association of Texas science teachers and diminutive earrings—both about 1/4 inch in size. The biggest Texas images are best seen from the air. Rumor has it that the Perry-Castañeda Library at the University of Texas at Austin is shaped like the state, and a glimpse of the building from the air confirms that it could be creatively interpreted as such by those who see Texas in distorted cruciform shapes. Golfers at the Four Seasons Resort and Club in Las Colinas find

FIG. 2-25. An advertisement for the London showing of the musical, "The Best Little Whorehouse in Texas," popularly portrays Texas in a racy or bawdy manner. (Courtesy Richard Meyer)

FIG. 2-26. This logo for the Knee and Sports Medicine Institute of Texas in Arlington conveys speed and power. (Courtesy Knee and Sports Medicine Institute)

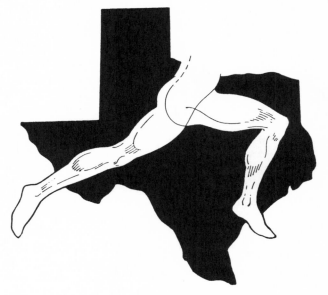

FIG. 2-28. In Corsi-
cana, Texas, a Texas-
shaped planter made
out of logs surrounds
a tree stump that ap-
pears to mark the
location of Corsicana
on a map. (1992
photo by author)

themselves playing on a large Texas-shaped green (a nearby sand trap is in
the shape of Oklahoma) (fig. 2-29). However, to understand that geographic
fact requires a different orientation: they have to gaze widely and have a
good sense of spatial proportions to recognize that they are literally playing
in Texas.

The largest outline maps of Texas are found in rural areas and are best
seen from the air. In East Texas, a farmer near Rockwall created a large map-
shaped farm pond about 250 feet long, "to let folks know he's fond of living
in Texas" (fig. 2-30).[10] One can only imagine the reaction that this vernacular earthwork gets from air travelers flying into and out of the Dallas–Fort
Worth Metroplex. In West Texas, a large grouping of trees locals call the
Trees of Texas was created by Midland farmer Wiley W. Walls in the 1940s.
Air photographs reveal the map to be about 400 feet wide. Since Wall's death
in 1966, this Texas-shaped grove of trees (including elms, pears, peaches,
sugar maples, Arizona cypress, and mulberries) has become rather disheveled,
but it remains a remarkable "natural area."[11] This is, to my knowledge, the

FIG. 2-29. This graphic prepared by the Four Seasons Resort and Club at Las Colinas, near Dallas, depicts a distinctive design feature of the Cottonwood Valley course by Robert Trent Jones, Jr. A Texas-shaped green is bordered by an Oklahoma-shaped sand trap. (Author's collection)

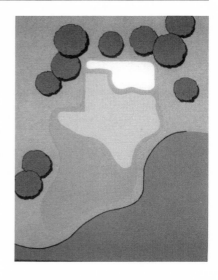

FIG. 2-30. A farmer created this correctly oriented Texas-shaped pond near Rockwall as a demonstration of his love of the state. (1993 photo by author)

largest map of Texas ever made, but somewhere, a few informants have said, a farmer must have plowed the boundaries of a huge pasture or field—say, about a section, or square mile, of land—in the shape of Texas or planted a Texas-shaped map in contrasting crops or flowers, such as bluebonnets and Indian paintbrush. That apocryphal landscape probably does not exist; however, it would be a perfect way of using the state map to convey a sense of the Lone Star State—Texas—as territory with a shape that no one could, or would, dare to dispute.

PLATE 1. The rather accurate but stylized map and the pictographic symbols on this postcard convey a message that is both educational and recreational. (Courtesy School Mart, San Antonio, Texas)

PLATE 2. This postcard uses the map quite effectively, and humorously, to illustrate Texans' attitudes about the size of their state in relation to the rest of the country. Note that although the state's shape is distorted, it is still easily recognizable as Texas. (Courtesy A-W Distributors and Importers, Irving, Texas)

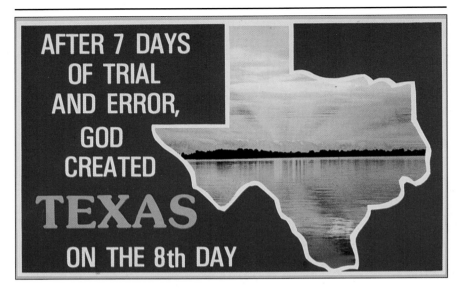

AFTER 7 DAYS
OF TRIAL
AND ERROR,
GOD
CREATED
TEXAS
ON THE 8th DAY

PLATE 3. This postcard combines two graphic devices—the state map and landscape imagery—to equate Texas with Eden. (Courtesy A-W Distributors and Importers, Irving, Texas)

PLATE 4. "The Eyes of Texas" compact features Texas-themed makeup, such as Tumbleweed and Yellow Rose, in compartments that are reminiscent of county outlines on a state map. (HC International Trade, Inc.; courtesy University of Texas at Arlington)

PLATE 5. Sign for the Republic of Texas restaurant, located on the River Walk in San Antonio, uses the map and star to convey a sense of Texas history and patriotism. (1991 photo by author)

PLATE 6. The cover of *Arts and Letters Clip Art Handbook for Computers* subtly incorporates a Texas map as part of its artwork. (Courtesy Computer Support Corporation, Dallas, Texas)

PLATE 7. The Texas Hot Dog Company facade at the Parks Mall in Arlington reveals subtle bas-relief maps of Texas. (1991 photo by author)

PLATE 8. Automobile dealer David McDavid's 1992 advertisement in Dallas–Fort Worth area newspapers uses the map as a flaming cattlebrand to generating an instant, almost visceral response and a recognition of the dealership as a Texas enterprise. (Courtesy David McDavid, Irving, Texas)

PLATE 9. Lone Star Pasta noodles in the shape of Texas are found in many Texas kitchens. (Photo by author)

PLATE 10. A familiar graphics theme—Texas in action and motion—takes on a personality in this postcard image promoting Texas tourism. (Courtesy A-W Distributor and Importers, Irving, Texas)

PLATE 11. A Texas map is transformed into a poignant symbol when embroidered into the AIDS memorial quilt as a way of remembering those who died of the disease. This quilt panel is from the AIDS quilt names project, Portland, Oregon. (Courtesy Richard Meyer)

PLATE 12. Wilhelm Reitnauer's horse head crystal artwork reveals a touch of Texas, as seen in the Texas map in the bridle and bit. (Courtesy Wilhelm Reitnauer)

PLATE 13. A partial map is part of a business sign in Arlington. Although approximately 50 percent of the outline is obscured by lettering, one can still recognize the map as Texas. (1991 photo by author)

PLATE 14. Among the most deconstructed Texas maps is that used in the Gibraltar Savings logo, shown here on a storefront in Memphis, Texas. Note that approximately 70 percent of the border is missing, yet the resulting image still reads as Texas. A portion of the Panhandle and the Rio Grande border remain as important identifying features. (1991 Photo by author)

PLATE 15. The map in the Institute of Texan Cultures logo employs a powerful diagonal design. The silhouettes or profiles serve to promote Texas' multicultural heritage. (Courtesy Institute of Texan Cultures)

PLATE 16. A silhouette map confirming Euless as part of Texas is reminiscent of the Welcome to Texas monuments erected at the state's borders. (1993 photo by author)

PLATE 17. An interesting map graphic on the side of a commercial building in Italy, Texas, combines two familiar maps (Texas and Italy) and urges a drug-free community. (1992 photo by author)

PLATE 18. Adopted during the period of the Texas Republic (1836–45), the Texas flag, which uses a star to symbolize Texas independence, remains a powerful symbol of Texas identity. (Courtesy Special Collections Division, The University of Texas at Arlington Libraries)

PLATE 19. The Lone Star has gradually yielded to the Texas map its status as the design most commonly identified with "Texas." Although a star does appear in this 1991 logo of the Lone Star Trolley Company in San Antonio, it is the map that forms the dominant image. This logo appears on the sides of the motorized "trolley cars" that transport tourists around the city. (Photo by author)

PLATE 20. This sign for the Texas State Square at Fiesta Texas theme park in San Antonio features the flag complete with star and red, white, and blue tricolors in the shape of the Texas map. (1992 photo by author)

PLATE 21. Texas as America? Judging from this stenciled marking on a load of Louisiana Pacific lumber, someone has interpreted Texas as the United States. To many proud Texans, being a Texan is more American than simply being an American from any other state, and this image therefore would not present a contradiction. (1991 photo by author)

PLATE 22. This poster for a 1951 Universal Pictures drama used an oddly shaped pink Texas map, along with western and rural imagery to promote the motion picture. (Author's collection)

PLATE 23. Not only by day but also by night, the map of Texas is a prominent image. Beer signs like this one are among the most common. (1992 photo by author)

PLATE 24. Regionalism in neon: This gift shop in Goliad uses a Texas outline map with an outline heart to attract visitors. (1992 photo by author)

PLATE 25. Rural Texas: Gateway entrance to the Harmony Meadows Ranch near Tehuacana, Limestone County, features a Texas map and images of the state flower. (1992 photo by author)

PLATE 26. This lawn lighting display, built by Marcus Roy of Fort Worth on his father's front lawn in Arlington, exemplifies Texans' ability to be humorous and serious about the state simultaneously. (1992 photo by author)

PLATE 27. The ultimate Texas map appears on the stage during the finale of a musical show at the Fiesta Texas theme park in San Antonio. (Courtesy Fiesta Texas)

3.
The Creation of an Icon

The map of Texas reminds me of our fight for independence from Mexico at the
Alamo, Goliad, and San Jacinto.
                                            —a grade school teacher in Dallas, Texas

THE MAP OF TEXAS HAS BECOME A POPULAR ICON THAT INSTANTLY SAYS
"Texas" as well as, or perhaps better than, "traditional" Texas popular
imagery such as the Lone Star, armadillos, oil wells, ten-gallon hats, and
longhorn cattle. As we have seen, the map of Texas is used to advertise thousands of Texas-owned and -operated businesses, products, and services. The
average Texan sees the map outline hundreds, perhaps thousands, of times
every day—on license plates, billboards, food product advertisements, and
jewelry. The map outline helps integrate time (history) and place (geography) in the popular mind, and it is easy to assume that the map of Texas has
always been shaped as we see it today.

The Texas map conveys a sense of history that has found its way into
America's popular culture. In an episode of "The Simpsons" that first aired
on April 25, 1991, substitute teacher Mr. Bergstrom pretends to be a Great
Plains cowboy from the 1830s and challenges the students to tell him what is
wrong with the cowboy outfit he is wearing. Lisa Simpson quickly reels off
the answers. One pertains to Bergstrom's Texas-shaped belt buckle, which,
Lisa tells him, "can't be correct, because Texas didn't become a state until
1845." Lisa Simpson is something of a child genius, but historians of cartography would have to correct her because Bergstrom's belt buckle could not
date from 1845, even though Texas was annexed at that time; the current
shape of Texas dates from 1850. It took the Mexican War (and several other
adjustments) to yield the present outline.

Evolution of the Texas Map

How did the map of Texas evolve? In the beginning, of course, there was no
"Texas" as a geopolitical entity, but only a diverse geographic area that was

occupied by dozens of Native American tribes such as the Karankawa and Towankonis. These peoples used the physical parameters, such as rivers, hills, and the coastline, to define their territories. The Gulf Coast formed a primordial boundary, a curve of sand spits and islands on which Spanish explorers—including Alvar Núñez Cabeza de Vaca and his shipwrecked fellow survivors—first made contact with the natives in 1534. Into this Gulf Coast flowed major rivers—the Bravo, Nueces, Brazos, Colorado, Trinity, and Sabine—that were explored by the French and the Spanish. It was these rivers that were to become the Europeans', and later the Americans', first significant boundary lines. By the late 1600s, the word "Tejas" began to be used to describe the natives as well as the place. By the early 1700s, the area was claimed by Spain, but its borders were vague, defined as much by natural features as by the shifting western boundaries of New France (fig. 3-1).[1]

Inland from the distinctive coastline, the land mass of Texas rises almost imperceptibly at first, then in a series of steplike cuestas, finally to ranges of hills and mountains far from the Gulf of Mexico. This huge area came under Spanish control and had boundaries that fluctuated, depending on the political conditions in New Spain. It was part of Nuevo Santander, San Luis Potosí, Nuevo León, Tamaulipas, and Tejas. Always a marginal frontier area of New Spain,[2] Texas became part of a much larger province—Coahuila y Tejas—after the French threat ended in the 1760s. Although New Spain had claimed the land as far east as the Mississippi River with the Louisiana Purchase of 1803 and the Adams-Onís Treaty of 1819, the eastern boundary of Texas was finally established at the Sabine River, a rather enduring "political" boundary we still recognize. Under its short tenure as a state of the Republic of Mexico (1821–36) Texas was colonized by former Americans taking advantage of Mexico's liberal *empresario* system. That system led to the division of the settled eastern portion of Texas into colonies during what D.W. Meinig calls the period of implantation.[3]

By the early to mid 1830s, Texas had slipped from the hands of the Mexican government as Anglo Americans became the majority. The Texas Revolution of 1836 resulted in a republic whose boundaries were disputed by Mexico: Texas claimed the Río Bravo (Rio Grande) as its southwestern border while Mexico claimed the Nueces River; Texas claimed a long appendage that included all the country to, and including, the headwaters of the Rio Grande and Arkansas River in what is today Colorado and, on some maps, today's Wyoming. This appendage was disputed by New Mexicans, who resented the arrogance of Texas claims to an area—what we today call the Hispano Homeland—that had been settled more than a century before Texas. This oddly shaped, defiant empire or republic (fig. 3-2) was best represented not by a map but by a star that symbolized its independence.

Even after Texas joined the United States in 1845, Mexico continued to dispute the Lone Star State's claims. This led, in part, to the Mexican War of

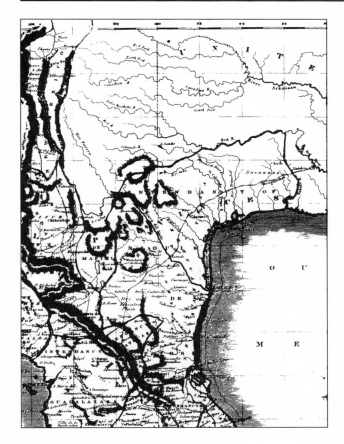

FIG. 3-1. Under Spain, and later Mexico, Texas was a province on the northern frontier, or *norte*. A detail of an 1810 D. Lizars map of Mexico and Guatemala shows what would later become Texas as a part of the intendancy of San Luis Potosi. (Courtesy Special Collections Division, University of Texas at Arlington Libraries)

1846–48, which still did not resolve the question of how much territory belonged to Texas, or what the shape of Texas should be. The Compromise of 1850—which found Texas keeping its Rio Grande frontier at El Paso but seeing its northwestern section dissected into the distinctive Panhandle, which was bounded by New Mexico on the west and the Indian Territory (Oklahoma) on the north and east—found Texas taking the shape we recognize today. Significantly, the U.S. government, not Texans, determined the shape of Texas that we recognize today.

Three aspects of the shape are readily apparent: it is about as wide as it is tall; it is roughly cruciform or star-shaped; and it consists of wavy or irregular natural borders on its eastern perimeter and rectangular borders on its northwestern perimeter. This last factor reminds us that Texas is both an eastern state (a substantial portion of East Texas was surveyed using the early metes and bounds technique) and a western state (the western portion

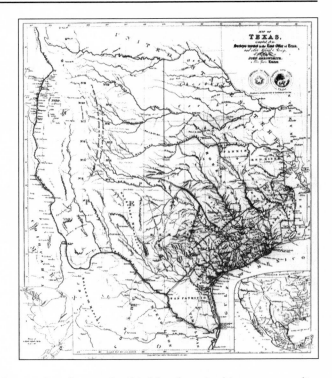

FIG. 3-2. John Arrowsmith's 1844 map of the Texas Republic reveals a huge area of ungainly shape. Borders on maps during the Texas Republic (1836–45) vary, for Texas was able to defend only the eastern portion of the Republic, and New Mexico disputed its claims to the western lands. (Courtesy Special Collections Division, University of Texas at Arlington Libraries)

was surveyed using the rectangular methods). Nowhere is this east-west distinction better seen than in the shape of Texas' counties. The earliest (eastern) counties are irregular and arranged in a "crazy quilt" pattern, whereas the western counties are square and orthogonally (compass) oriented. Geopolitically, the morphology of Texas tells us much about the history of the state's colonization and settlement.

Even though it had been whittled down, the resulting land mass was the largest state at the time, and was to remain so until the admission of Alaska in 1959. While 1850 would seem to mark the year in which Texas as we know it officially took final form, one sees some maps that have a protuberance at the southeast corner of the Panhandle (fig. 3-3), which protrudes into what we know today as Oklahoma. This is the disputed Greer County, claimed by Texas until the U.S. Supreme Court's 1899 ruling that Oklahoma's claims—not those of Texas—were valid.

Ever since Texas achieved its overall shape in the mid nineteenth century, it has suffered when being represented on a rectangular sheet of paper. The Panhandle, in particular, has been treated with indifference by some cartographers, who have placed it in a corner after severing it from the main portion of the map. Early examples show that by the early 1850s Texas could be

FIG. 3-3. Most maps of Texas following the Compromise of 1850 show the state as we know it today. However, this 1875 map by J. Bartholomew of Edinburgh includes the disputed Greer County between the forks of the Red River—an area which the U.S. Supreme Court later ruled belonged to Oklahoma Territory. (Courtesy Special Collections Division, University of Texas at Arlington Libraries)

represented in dismembered form (fig. 3-4). The western and occasionally the southern tips have suffered such treatment, too, but more rarely than the Panhandle, leading one to wonder whether such treatment has encouraged the Panhandle to threaten secession on occasion and to be named, paradoxically, "Old Texas" (even though it is arguably the youngest part of the state). Despite numerous attempts to divide Texas into two or more smaller states, such as the aggressive efforts of Reconstruction politicians to create the state of West Texas in 1868–69,[4] Texas has remained intact. Thus, the map reaffirms that Texans' nineteenth-century political struggles to keep the state intact were successful.

Whatever else we may say about the evolution of Texas and its map in the mid to late nineteenth century, however, one must acknowledge mapmakers' growing confidence in their ability to accurately depict the state's shape. Most maps of the time are easily recognized as Texas. However, there are exceptions. Because longitude was difficult to calculate accurately until about 1860, some maps compress or squeeze the state, especially the western portion. Thus, mapmakers continually produced "new and correct" maps of Texas that had, indeed, become more correct by about 1900. We must remember that cartographers produced inaccurate maps because they often simply copied earlier maps. Cartography is both an art and a science, and it evolved slowly until the age of sophisticated surveying. Nowhere is that seen more clearly than in the seemingly endless process of achieving accuracy—that of "fine tuning" the map we recognize today as Texas.

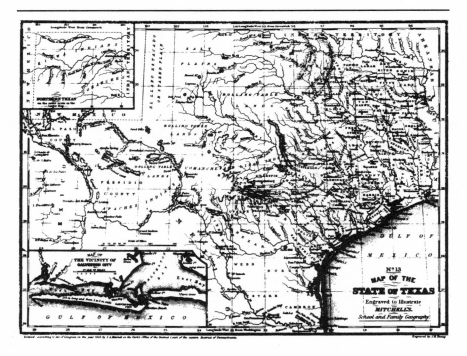

FIG. 3-4. Cartographers have often dismembered Texas when depicting it on a rectangular sheet of paper. The Panhandle is the most frequent casualty, although the southern and western tip might also be disembodied. This 1852 map from *Mitchell's School Atlas*, was published by Thomas Cowperthwait and Company, Philadelphia. (Courtesy Special Collections Division, University of Texas at Arlington)

Projecting the Map of Texas

Up to this point, we have considered the shape of Texas in relation to two types of points of reference that are more or less fixed: (1) natural features, such as rivers, which occasionally meander into new channels (but surveys of whose earlier courses remain to determine boundaries); and (2) arbitrary, fixed lines of longitude and latitude that may be invisible on the landscape but that dictate the perimeter. In the case of the former, we may say that the Rio Grande serves as the boundary but we realize that, in the interests of harmony, the border may be a dry channel where the river has shifted course; and in the latter, we may speak of the northern border of Texas being the parallel at 36 degrees 30 minutes north latitude and the western border of the Panhandle being the straight line at 103 degrees west longitude. Thus, Texas is bounded by physical geographic features as well as geometric abstract lines that serve to divide up the globe.

And that leads us to an interesting conclusion about all maps of Texas:

they all can be accurate only to a point because, like all maps, they attempt to depict part of a sphere on a flat surface (such as a piece of paper or, in the case of many Texas maps, flat signs). In order to represent Texas on a flat surface, the map has to be at least slightly distorted. For example, the two north-south lines delineating the width of the Texas Panhandle (the legendary 100th meridian on the east and 103 degrees longitude on the west) are not really parallel, because these lines of longitude converge at the North Pole; nevertheless, many maps represent them as parallel lines even though they would not be parallel if drawn on the surface of the earth.

There are many different ways of representing portions of the round earth on flat surfaces; cartographers call them map projections.[5] In the case of a map showing the Panhandle as having perfectly parallel lines, the cartographer uses a projection that simply disregards the curvature of the earth and the convergence of lines of longitude at the poles (i.e., a Mercator projection). Such a map is technically inaccurate, but certainly good enough to serve most purposes. Yet, it does distort Texas slightly from its real shape.

Even various governmental agencies in Texas used different map projections until very recently, when the differences became a liability because highly detailed and very accurate mapping based on Geographic Information Systems (GIS) technology requires consistency.[6] A statewide committee chaired by Stephen Shackelford of the Texas Department of Transportation analyzed the pros and cons of the major map projections in 1992, and settled on a Lambert conformal conic projection, as represented in figure 3-5. This Texas State Plan Coordinate System map represents an "optimal approach," which "will help to facilitate map usability, thereby helping to reduce overall state GIS costs."[7] After its adoption in 1993, Texas agencies had a standard map image of the state.

As we shall see, most Texans have no difficulty recognizing the map of Texas; they can distinguish it from other state maps almost without fail. And yet, because there is such a lack of integration between history and geography, many Texans do not know what period of time the state map depicts. If, as we have seen, the map image of Texas is basically post-1850, many Texans simply are not aware of that fact. In fact, a Dallas teacher informed me that "the reason the map of Texas is such a good symbol for Texas is because it reminds us Texans of the Texas Republic." Another informant, surprised to learn that the map dated not from the Texas Republic but from early statehood, responded, "Why, I thought we always used the map of Texas along with the Lone Star [as Texas symbols]." This kind of thinking is a logical outcome of a culture that considers geography and history to be separate subjects.

Given the changing shape of Texas from the 1830s to 1850, we are left with an interesting design enigma: the *current* Texas map would have made a fine graphic symbol during the Republic had it been available; now that it

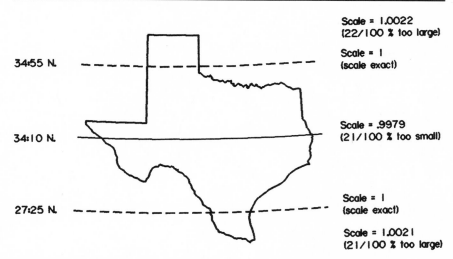

Scale = 1.0022
(22/100 % too large)

Scale = 1
(scale exact)

Scale = .9979
(21/100 % too small)

Scale = 1
(scale exact)

Scale = 1.0021
(21/100 % too large)

34:55 N.

34:10 N.

27:25 N.

FIG. 3-5. The official map of Texas, adopted for Geographic Information Systems (GIS) use in 1992, employs a Lambert Conformal Conic projection. Like all maps, it represents a compromise in depicting a curving surface on a flat plane, but is more accurate than many others. (Courtesy Stephen Shackelford, Texas Department of Transportation)

is available, it serves successfully (if incorrectly) in the popular mind as a symbol that should have existed historically. Maps have the power to convey myth as well as truth, and have been used for millennia to do both.

Thanks to aggressive promotion, the resulting post-1850 (or, officially, post-1899) map of Texas has become America's most recognizable state map. Its recognizability goes beyond Texans; many Americans recognize the outline instantly, because, as a student in Kentucky opined, "no other state has a shape that even remotely resembles Texas." At the height of the Persian Gulf Crisis, a 1991 episode of "Saturday Night Live" used the outline of Texas to humorous advantage. The producers substituted a map of Texas and identified it as the Middle East, to roars of laughter—perhaps an oblique reference to then–President George Bush's "line in the sand" message to Saddam Hussein, a message that had subtle connections to the Battle of the Alamo. After years of exposure to the map of Texas, the public instantly recognizes its shape. In fact, many people can actually draw it (or approximations of it) from memory. How they do so reveals much about the map's power as an icon.

Drawing the Texas Map

Consider the challenge: You are given a blank piece of paper and asked to draw a map of Texas from memory. Before you begin, however, you must do two things at almost the same time—visualize both the *perimeter* (that is, the

FIG. 3-6. Selected efforts by students in a University of Texas at Arlington history class to draw a map of Texas are shown here. Although they vary in size and outline, virtually all maps were recognizable as Texas by other students, and included the major elements—a tip, bulge, and panhandle. (Author's collection)

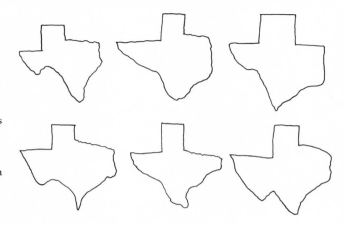

shape or outline) and the *massing* of the interior of the seemingly empty space you will enclose. These tasks must be done almost simultaneously because where the lines of an outline are drawn depends on conceptualizing the interior form of the object drawn. In other words, drawing an outline of something as complex as Texas demands that one must implicitly recognize the differing volumes of the space enclosed.

To see how well people might handle the task, I asked my history students at the University of Texas at Arlington to perform it. The students tended to do rather well; that is, they could produce maps that, for the most part, were immediately recognizable as Texas by others in the class. Looking at several of their responses (fig. 3-6) reveals several facts about the way the map is conceptualized by the public:

> 1. *Simplified perimeter.* We know that Texas is bordered by some very complex natural features, such as the Rio Grande, the Red River, and the Gulf Coast. Many students reproduced these portions of the outline, but simplified them in doing so. Although the minute details of the perimeter help give Texas its character, the task of remembering every bend in, say, the Red River or every barrier island along the coast, is impossible for the average person; nevertheless, people do know that the perimeter consists of several very different shapes, and they draw them in a simplified manner that retains at least enough of the distinctive morphology to differentiate them from other parts of the outline. For example, the Rio Grande is depicted often as two or three broad sinuous curves that snake along the southwestern perimeter of the map, while the Panhandle is square or rectangular—or as nearly square or rectangular as people can draw it.

2. *Accurate proportions.* The basic width-to-height ratio of the map was depicted fairly accurately. As we have seen, Texas is slightly wider than it is tall (i.e., 97 percent as tall as it is wide). The students' maps respected the proportions. Their maps averaged 5.03 inches wide by 4.95 inches tall (ca. 97 percent). This surprising fidelity reminds us of the overall power of the Texas map as a graphic. The fact that it is fundamentally a distorted cross or star in most people's minds may ensure its being depicted with fairly "correct" proportions.

3. *Distorted but recognizable massing.* Nevertheless, Texas has a complicated outline that is very difficult to recall exactly. Most of the students sketched out the two axes (north-south and east-west) that are defined by the southern tip, the Panhandle, West Texas, and East Texas; they knew that the Rio Grande border and the Gulf Coast meet at the southern tip, but had considerable trouble visualizing, and hence drawing, the relationship correctly. Likewise they knew that the Panhandle was square, but most had some difficulty placing it in relation to the large, crenulated mass or bulge of northeastern Texas. Asking them to draw the map required that they place the distinctive elements of the perimeter in proper position—which is no easy task in the case of Texas. Nevertheless, most students produced an image whose massing is recognizable as Texas, although they apologized for their maps' "inaccuracy." This is understandable. The very things that make the map of Texas recognizable (distinctive radiant form based on complex shapes and asymmetrical massing) also make it difficult to reproduce accurately. This is the very factor, of course, that makes Texas such a distinctive symbol: it is a unique image that is easy to recognize but difficult to counterfeit.

When asked to describe the actual process they used in drawing the map, many students responded that they began with the "most familiar" part of the outline (often the southern tip or the Panhandle) and began to draw it with reference to where they visualized the other important elements to be. In so doing, they often considered the entire sheet of paper as their field, but were careful to center the resulting map on the page. In other words, this exercise reaffirms that when a map is conceptualized, the interplay between perimeter and massing is essential. Getting it to their satisfaction found several students erasing earlier outlines, or drawing a light outline until the correct outline could be drawn darker.

These student maps reveal two very important aspects of popular cartography. First, like most mapmakers, the students drew planimetric maps (i.e., maps that are drawn looking straight down at the ground so that one's line of sight intersects the earth at a right angle); few would—or could—draw oblique maps (i.e., maps drawn with a view that intersects the earth at an angle, much the view one might see from an airplane or a spacecraft). Second, all of the students oriented their maps with north at the top. This conforms to our cultural perception, reinforced by cartographers in the western world for several centuries, that north is "up."

This assignment seemed to confirm that college students, at least those in my history courses, could certainly draw passable outline maps of Texas. But how would students in elementary school handle the same task? To answer this question, three classes of fourth graders at Saint Monica's School in Dallas were asked to draw the map of Texas from memory.[8] The results were surprising. These ten year olds produced maps that were almost as accurate as the maps their college-age counterparts had produced. A careful look at their responses (fig. 3-7) shows several trends that shed light on the process of how we learn about maps at an early age. The grade schoolers' maps were also oriented north and were drawn planimetrically, but revealed the following:

1. *Further simplification of the map perimeter.* These fourth-grade students tended to simplify or reduce the outline into abstract or geometrical shapes more than the college students had. In other words, they tended to reduce the complexity of the borders by drawing curved lines as straight lines instead of reproducing sinuous outlines. In the most extreme cases, for example, the Rio Grande and Red River borders have no detail at all, but are straight lines that run at the approximate angle of the prototype borders. In other cases, the sinuous lines were reduced to a series of more regularly spaced "waves," or small points and troughs that amount to serrations. These students knew that these portions of the outline were irregular, but were not certain about how they were configured, so they drew waving or ragged lines that regularized the edges.

2. *Further abstraction of perimeter and proportions.* The younger students had a greater tendency to reduce the complexity of the Texas map—some to the point of stylization. In reproducing the southern portions of the state (the Rio Grande and the coastline), for example, nearly 20 percent of the students drew two lines that converged at the tip. We might call this abstraction the "arrowhead phenomenon." In these maps the entire southern portion of the state is a simple downward-pointing triangle surmounted by a square, almost centrally positioned, Panhandle that reminds us of the base of an arrowhead. In its most simplified form, Texas appears to be a downward pointing arrowhead, but about 10 percent of the students also tended to abstract Texas into a cross shape, as can be seen in some of the student maps reproduced in figures 3-6 and 3-7. Fully 30

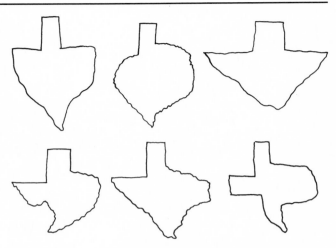

FIG. 3-7. Drawing the map of Texas from memory, three classes of 4th graders at Saint Monica's School in Dallas produced a wide range of shapes, including those shown here. Note the tendency to simplify the outline, as well as to produce an arrowhead shape. (Author's collection)

percent of the students, then, reproduced Texas as somewhat more symmetrical and simply shaped than it really is, and this helps us understand how people reduce or simplify complicated shapes by stylization.

3. *Consistency of proportions.* Although these grade school students tended to draw Texas slightly differently from the college students, both groups respected the state's width-to-height relationship. We might say that the most consistent aspect of the map exercise is that students tended to draw a shape that was about as wide as it was tall. A few students in both groups drew rather wide or tall Texas maps, and some of the younger students' maps were a bit more imaginative, but overall there was remarkable consistency regarding overall proportions. Surprisingly, the younger students' maps, too, respected Texas' 97:100 ratio of height to width.

Manipulating the Shape of Texas

These mapping exercises help demonstrate the inherent complexity of Texas and people's need to simplify its perimeter while inherently recognizing the most basic elements in its shape: Panhandle at the "top," acute angularity at the tip, and roughly cruciform shape with more heavy massing toward the east, all in a form whose perimeter is about as wide as it is tall.

That students are so adept at conceptualizing the map of Texas may be the result of an elementary cartography lesson taught in schools. Texas students learn from an early age that they carry a map of Texas with them at all times—their right hand. The thumb is West Texas, the upwardly extended index finger is the Panhandle, and the three remaining fingers form East Texas. This device was immortalized in Townsend Miller's "A Letter from

Texas," first published in 1939 by Dallas-based Neiman Marcus. In it, a friend tries to describe the shape, immensity, and diversity of Texas:

> John it is a strange land. John it is hard to describe.
> But perhaps like this: hold up your right hand, palm outward
> And break the last three fingers down from the joint
> And there I think you have it. The westering thumb
> The beautiful bleak land, the silent mesas
> Big Bend and the great canyons and at its end
> El Paso, the Northern Pass, and they came down through it.
> Southward and east the slow hot river moving
> River of Palms, Grande del Norte, and over the wrist
> To Brownsville and it empties in the vast blue waters.
> Upward the long coast curving and far above it
> Over the bent joints the red bordering river
> Red River, land of the Washita and Tejas
> And last the index, Panhandle, the high plains
> The bleached bone laid on the huge heart of the continent.
> This is the empire; this is the hand flung out
> The large western dream and the tongue staggers
> To speak it for the size or where to take it.[9]

We have seen that drawing the map of Texas from memory normally involves taking certain liberties, namely, simplification and abstraction. Most of us, however, never have to draw a map at all, and those who do produce a map of Texas for, say, an advertisement or a logo, will trace it from an authoritative source—a road map or another map that in turn has been drawn from a "mother" map. As one businessman in Austin told me, he "simply used a state road map to ensure accuracy" in creating a logo for his company.

And yet, not all Texas maps are accurately proportioned or outlined. Take, for example, the AFL-CIO silhouette map of Texas used on the union's logo (fig. 3-8). It reproduces a common error—the tip is too narrow and suspiciously reminiscent of the tip of South America. Much the same "error" is seen on the sign proudly erected by the Electra Tigers High School football team; the tip has a slight reverse curve and is narrow (fig. 3-9). And yet, the map of Texas is so recognizable that no one has much difficulty recognizing it even in some of its more distorted renditions. There is, then, a relationship between what we (as a group) draw and what we see—that is, we are fairly permissive about what we will accept as a Texas map. Generally, it needs only a Panhandle, a tip, a horn, and a bulge to qualify.

It should come as no surprise that the popular maps of Texas we encounter can contain many distortions and inaccuracies; after all, we tend to simplify and abstract complicated images all the time—as when a graphic of an

FIG. 3-8. Map of Texas embroidered on a banner of the AFL-CIO union in the 1940s. The southern tip is too narrow, but the map is readily recognized as Texas. (Courtesy Special Collections Division, University of Texas at Arlington Libraries)

FIG. 3-9. The Electra Tigers State Championship sign has a tip that curves too tightly and is too narrow and a simplified outline along the Red River; but it, too, is easily recognized as a map of Texas. (1991 photo by author)

automobile is reduced to a semicircular blob (the car's body) that rests on two circles (wheels). We recognize it as an automobile whether or not we know which (if any) part is the front or the back. Much the same kind of visual simplification occurs with the map of Texas, even to the point that the map is recognizable as a reverse (or mirror) image.

Consider, for example, the fascinating cover of *The Dictionary of Texas Misinformation* by Anne Dingus (fig. 3-10). The designer has creatively used a play on graphics by reversing the map image. This helps prepare the reader for a series of revelations about popularly held (but incorrect) information about Texas. The map's reversal in this context implies erroneous information, and yet the fact that the map is still recognizable reveals an important concept, namely, that the information can be erroneous but still constitute an important part of popular stereotypes about Texas. The more carefully we study this reverse image, the more we come to understand the power of the shape of the Texas map. Looking at this mirror image helps us better understand that the personality or character of the shape of Texas, like that of a human face, is asymmetrical.

This juxtaposition of visual symmetry and asymmetry has been used by advertisers who reverse the Texas map image as a way of capturing our attention (fig. 3-11). When we see such maps, our minds instantly begin to unscramble the image; that is, we know we have seen it often, but we cannot completely recognize it until we make the effort to reorient it. In some ways, much the same process occurs when we rearrange incorrectly placed letters in a misspelled word. Studying these reversed maps helps us understand that visual images, such as maps, are part of our vocabulary.

As we encounter Texas maps in a wide variety of settings, we note another design feature: upside-down maps. The distinctive form of Texas is creatively manipulated to symbolize recycling in one graphic that inverts one map (fig. 3-12), while the ultimate in inversion appears to be the familiar Texas Stone paving blocks in the shape of Texas. With some careful and creative alteration of the Texas map, Texas Stone has designed maps that are correct when viewed from either direction (fig. 3-13). Products like the Texas Stone reveal how adaptable the Texas map is to graphic design, how roughly symmetrical the basic shape of the state is, and how ingenious product designers are in using it.

Deconstructing Texas

Taking the theme of visual order and disorder a step farther, we may be surprised at how often portions of the Texas map, or its perimeter, are actually omitted in graphic advertising. I call these maps "deconstructed" in that parts are either missing (plate 13), or the map is fragmented into several sections or pieces (fig. 3-14). Such maps are quite manipulative, one might

FIG. 3-10. Displaying a reversal of the map image that beautifully conveys the subject of the book, the cover of *Texas Misinformation* reveals that we can still recognize the map image even though it appears backwards. (Courtesy Gulf Publishing Co.)

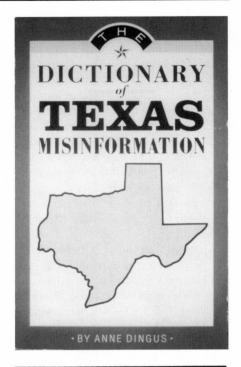

FIG. 3-11. The reversal of Texas maps seen in this 1992 advertisement for a San Antonio gun show is particularly effective. Do the maps subliminally substitute for two holstered handguns, as one informant suggested? Note that only one word, Texas, is reversed on the silhouette map image. (Courtesy *San Antonio Express*)

FIG. 3-12. Recycling Centers of Texas uses an interesting and very effective combination of two maps, one correct, the other inverted, in a 1991 advertisement to convey the recycling theme. (Reproduced with permission of Southwestern Bell Yellow Pages, Inc.; all rights reserved)

FIG. 3-13. Texastone patio pavers by Pavestone feature an ingenious design, as seen in this pathway at the Fort Worth Zoo. (Photo by author; assisted by Frank Duty and Mike Polson)

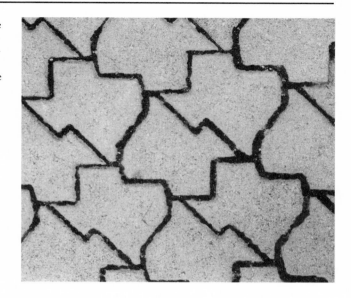

FIG. 3-14. The map of Texas may be manipulated or distorted to convey action, change, or speed. In this 1991 advertisement the map of Texas is shaped by several powerful horizontal lines, and the southern tip has been completely eliminated. (Reproduced with permission of Southwestern Bell Yellow Pages, Inc.; all rights reserved)

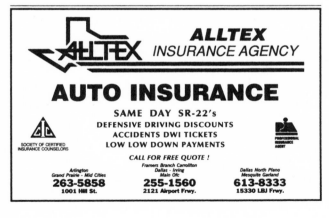

also say playful, in that they result in decidedly enticing and risky graphic designs that further stimulate our interest and curiosity.

We might ask two questions about such deconstructed maps: (1) Just how much can one subtract from the perimeter and still say the map represents Texas (i.e., what percentage needs to remain to be recognizable)? (2) What parts of the outline are more, or less, dispensable (i.e., what parts can be omitted and still yield a recognizable map)?

Answering these questions requires that we look at hundreds of Texas maps that are representative of all the Texas map outlines we see daily. What better place to find them than in the Southwestern Bell Yellow Pages, which feature a wealth of advertising logos and graphics that identify products and services. David Filewood analyzed Texas map images in the Yellow Pages from twenty Texas cities. This involved searching through more than twenty-one thousand pages. Filewood notes that fully 39 percent of the Texas maps featured obscured borders; that is, the map outline was interrupted by other content, such as a written slogan (e.g., "The best buys in Texas") or an illustration (e.g., an automobile or an armadillo). Filewood also discovered that 15 percent of the maps were fragmented, which is to say, the geographic shape of Texas was broken into two or more sections, or "deconstructed" for impact or effect.

What portions of Texas are likely to be preserved—or eliminated—when the map is deconstructed? My study of student maps implies that certain portions are essential, and popular mapmakers apparently agree. Filewood found that of the maps having only partial borders, 92 percent featured the southern tip, 84 percent featured the Panhandle, and 66 percent used the Rio Grande. These aspects of the maps, we will recall, are most readily drawn by respondents. This reaffirms that the tip, the Panhandle, and the Rio Grande appear to be the most important parts of the outline; the Red River, eastern (Sabine River) border, and coastline are important in the composite image but secondary in conveying the initial image of Texas. Although the tip, the Panhandle, and the Rio Grande constitute about 50 percent of the outline, they are the most important elements in conveying a cartographic image of Texas.

On occasion, one entire crucial element, such as the tip, can be eliminated; the remainder is so recognizable that it can still be identified as Texas. This reminds us that as little as 35 percent of the outline can be used to convey Texas in some advertisements. Among the most interesting is the First Gibraltar Savings logo, which features only one part of the Panhandle and the Rio Grande border (plate 14). As we saw in chapter 2, the cruciform shape of Texas is sometimes manipulated into the letter T, especially a lower-cased t. Tejas Shooting Sports of Odessa very creatively uses a partial map of the state, as well as the star, for its logo (fig. 3-15); the Panhandle and the southwestern border are so recognizable that they suffice to create a deconstructed but acceptable map of Texas.

Deconstruction, then, can take two forms: (1) the actual removal or absence of a part of the massing or perimeter of the Texas map, as when *Texas Highways* magazine used a very sketchy map of Texas in a questionnaire to readers (fig. 3-16) or when the Texas Music Association employed a bisected silhouette map straddling a music note (fig. 3-17); or (2) the obscuring of the perimeter by another graphic that effectively covers part of Texas, as seen in Texas Television's striking advertisement in the El Paso Yellow Pages, in which only the Panhandle and the Red River borders remain in silhouette—and we

FIG. 3-15. A partial map—in this case the western half of the state—conveys a Texas identity in this 1991 advertisement. The (Lone) star dotting the "j" in Tejas reinforces a sense of place. (Reproduced with permission of Southwestern Bell Yellow Pages, Inc.; all rights reserved)

FIG. 3-16. A deconstructed image of the Texas map appears in a 1992 *Texas Highways* magazine questionnaire. This sketchy silhouette map demonstrates that the basic massing of the Texas map is as distinctive as its outline. (Art by Kelleygraphics; reprinted courtesy *Texas Highways*)

FIG. 3-17. The map in the Texas Music Association logo consists of two separate sections divided by a stylized musical note, yet it is easily recognized. Because both symbols are so identifiable, this graphic may be said to be a perfect visual transliteration for "Texas Music." (Courtesy Texas Music Association)

FIG. 3-18. Southwestern imagery abounds in this 1992 advertisement. The Texas map, or rather only part of it, is to the left representing a mesa or tableland as part of a regional landscape theme. (Reproduced with permission of Southwestern Bell Yellow Pages, Inc.; all rights reserved)

FIG. 3-19. Multiple map images of Texas often emphasize horizontality to imply action, as is the case with a graphic design on a Texas Trans Eastern tanker truck rolling through Texas on Interstate Highway 20. (1991 photo by Damien Francaviglia)

can still recognize Texas (fig. 3-18). This graphic is very interesting, for Texas becomes part of the landscape, reminding us, perhaps, of a mesa. Note, too, that it also features other reassuring "Texas" or western graphic imagery, including a star, a yucca, a cow skull, a longhorn face, and something that is often used to depict Texas but does not occur within three hundred miles of it—a saguaro cactus.

Here we enter a very important realm of Texas map use, namely, the placement of information on or over the map. About half of the Texas map advertisements use some kind of additional graphic device. In some cases, the results have been stunning. We recall the power of Billy Bob's name written boldly across the map of Texas. It uses a very common variation—a bold horizontal element that sprawls across the map.

If we analyze these supplemental graphic designs carefully, we find that most expand or widen the image of Texas, that is, stress its horizontality.

Subconsciously, there is good reason for this widening: most graphics that convey action are rectangular, that is, wider than they are tall. Consider the horizontal, rectangular format of a television or movie screen. The action sweeps across them. When we recall the position of Texas in the mythical geography of the nation, it is first as an east-west stage on which pioneering movement takes place. Those powerful horizontal Texas graphics may reinforce Texas' peculiar geographic position as a state that links the East (especially the Southeast) and the West (especially the Southwest). Some advertisers use this horizontality quite effectively by reproducing several overlapping Texas maps in one logo (fig. 3-19). We still recognize the state, for each map remains partially discrete, but the multiple overlapping reminds us of Texas expansionism and the inherent design instability of the Texas map.

This horizontality is supplemented by an exciting variation, namely, a diagonal banding of the graphics that seems to complement the empty spaces left in the niches created by the curve of the Gulf, the angle of the Rio Grande, or the void left where the Panhandle meets New Mexico. Consider, for example, the exciting and evocative logo of the Institute of Texan Cultures in San Antonio (plate 15). The complex outline/silhouette map of Texas is made all the more powerful as a graphic by the diagonal southwest to northeast banding that is surmounted by silhouettes of faces—each of which appears to have a different shape or ethnic character. This graphic emphasizes the multicultural heritage of Texas.

These diagonal graphics reveal a second major kinetic geographic/design thrust in the image of Texas, and they are a reminder that Texas had a tempestuous relationship with its neighbor to the south in the nineteenth century. Texas may in part be a southern state, but the presence of Mexico keeps it as a southwestern border state in our minds. With the passage of the North American Free Trade Agreement, which portends a tremendous increase in trade between the United States (Texas) and Mexico, one might expect to see this diagonal axis increase in popularity as a recognizable "frontier."

The persistence of these southwestern borders in graphics seems to confirm that Texas is a southern and western state in the popular mind. So, too, perhaps, does the common tendency to depict the map of Texas in relief—that is, as an actual piece or slice of land that has a bold edge, revealed by a shadow or lines that emphasize the geographic features of its southern, western, and southwestern borders (fig. 3-20). More than half of these relief maps emphasize the Rio Grande, the Panhandle, and the southern tip. The source of light in shadowed versions is most often from the north-northeast. This technique of north lighting (or northwest lighting) is commonly used in relief mapping, but in the case of Texas it takes on added significance because it emphasizes the perceptual defile that occurs at the border between the United States and Mexico; this further reminds us that Texas is a southern/ southwestern state.

FIG. 3-20. A billboard for Bluebonnet Ford on Interstate Highway 35 near New Braunfels, Texas, reveals several common features of Texas maps, including the use of graphic material (in this case the state flower) and the tendency to depict the state in relief. (1992 photo by author)

FIG. 3-21. The interesting sign welcoming motorists to Rio Vista, Texas, is made of metal and consists of an outline map upon which information about the town is conveyed. (1992 photo by author)

FIG. 3-22. This metal see-through sign marks the corporate limit of Turkey, Texas, home of country-swing pioneer Bob Wills. Intricate in design, it features country-western iconography in silhouette, including the Texas map, a windmill, cowboys, a fiddle, and musical notes. (1992 photo by author)

FIG. 3-23. This pink (Texas red) granite monument in front of the River Oaks city hall commemorates individuals and groups who contributed to the quality of life in the community. An official road map of Texas served as the pattern, according to monument maker Ron Henry, who is also shown. (1992 photo by author)

Usually, however, we see the map of Texas in its entirety, and that is when it has its full impact as an integrated and distinctive cartographic design. Significantly, deconstructed maps are most often seen when the viewer will have the time to interpret the image (for example, in newspaper advertisements and on the façades of commercial buildings in reduced speed zones). At higher speeds, when our cars may be passing by as quickly as 150 feet per second at 70 miles per hour, however, we have relatively little time for the luxury of reconstructing maps or other images and phrases. Thus, advertisers and designers need a high-impact graphic. If they want to say "Texas" in this type of situation, they use the entire state. Using the entire state also reaffirms the geographic connection, that is, Texas as place.

Among the most interesting of Texas maps are those three-dimensional relief maps that mark the entrances to communities. These provide the opportunity for a community to demonstrate that it is a viable part of the state—and to do so in the few seconds a motorist has to interact. First, the motorist sees the familiar shape of Texas that usually stands as a silhouette; next, the eye is drawn to the body of the map, where a star may mark the location; almost simultaneously, the name of the community is read in the context of a very short slogan or statement that may proclaim its friendliness, scenic attractions, or other claims to fame.

Texas-shaped welcome signs vary in size, materials, and message, but they are very revealing in what they say about a community. The rapidly growing community of Euless, located close to the Dallas–Fort Worth airport, uses a bold, simple silhouette map in stone (plate 16) to provide a welcome, while the small town of Rio Vista uses an ornate metal map that contains an outline map of the state and a substantial amount of narrative information about the community and its civic organizations (fig. 3-21). Among the most intriguing of the Texas-shaped welcoming signs are those erected for the small town of Turkey (fig. 3-22), home of country-swing music pioneer Bob Wills. Rendered in iron, the sign is actually a see-through device that encourages the motorist who has slowed to the reduced speed limit to experience simultaneously both the content of the sign and the rural landscape behind it. Signs like these often represent the best in county and regional communications techniques and remind the traveler that the map of Texas is a vital part of the rural Texas landscape.

Among the most interesting welcome signs is a Texas map painted on the side of a commercial building in the town of Italy (plate 17). In a play on graphics, a map of Italy (the country) is also juxtaposed, and the letters in the word "Italy" proclaim "*I*ndividuals *T*otally *A*gainst Drugs. *L*ove Yourself." This graphic, naturally, is in red, white, and green. Significantly, it reveals that even a small town can be affected by problems that were once considered urban. The Texas map is thus a familiar graphic in both rural and urban locations.

In town centers, one may find Texas-shaped markers in parks or in front of municipal buildings or town halls. These are often made of granite or metal (aluminum or bronze) and commemorate historic events or note the contributions of important people. Because the observer of these Texas-shaped maps is on foot and moving slowly, the marker is likely to contain a significant amount of narrative information. The commemorative marker situated in front of the River Oaks city hall is made of pink granite (fig. 3-23). The names of important townspeople were cut into the face of the stone by Fort Worth monument cutter Ron Henry. In order to get the Texas shape of the stone to correct proportions, Mr. Henry used a standard road map as a design template.[10]

In general, the more "official" a marker, the more likely its map is to be correctly proportioned. A study of cartographic techniques can tell us much about perceptions of, and attitudes toward, places. Maps are often associated with important narrations or textual materials about people and places in them. Using Roger Downs' analogy, we may say that the map serves as a metaphor for the content of place.[11] Although the word "metaphor" is normally associated with language, the analogy is appropriate. Maps, as we have seen, convey verbal as well as visual information and form part of a unified language incorporating words and pictures. In the case of Texas, it is impossible to separate map shape from symbolism and words about Texas from images. Moreover, because maps of Texas convey information about the personality of the state, and in so doing differentiate Texas from its neighbors, we may say that the Texas map becomes synonymous with Texas through symbolization. For Texans, as we have seen, the map has come to serve as an icon for the state's identity. In chapter 4, that identity will be considered in more detail, especially in light of the symbols that have been used to portray Texans as a people. The fact that Texans embrace the map as their symbol is not surprising, but, as we shall see, the map is just one of the symbols that have served to identify Texas through time. How it has emerged as the premier symbol of Texas in the 1990s is the subject of our next chapter.

4.
From Map to Symbol

Maps . . . are the most abstract form of didactic substitute imagery.
                                            —Alan Gowans, *Learning to See*

TEXANS, OF COURSE, HAVE HAD MANY SYMBOLS THAT SERVE TO IDENTIFY THEIR state. Whereas the present shape of Texas may be considered an artifact of Texas' statehood and compromise—as we saw in chapter 3—the state's identity predates the Anglo American presence. As David Weber has noted, the forced combination of Coahuila y Tejas under Mexican rule was a source of considerable tension and led to agitation for separation.[1] As Anglo influence became more dominant in the 1820s and early 1830s, and as the threat of revolt from Mexico became more tangible, Texas' identity became more defiant. Successful revolution was precipitated by the Anglos, who received considerable support from Tejanos fed up with the seemingly tyrannical rule of General Antonio López de Santa Anna. Nevertheless, most of the iconography associated with Texas independence is Anglo. An early Anglo flag associated with the Battle of Goliad features a cannon with the simple words, "Come and take it."

What has been interpreted as a purely Anglo American victory because Sam Houston's troops defeated the Mexican army at San Jacinto in East (Anglo) Texas was, in part and in reality, a victory that could be shared by Mexican Tejanos who supported the independence of Texas. For more than 150 years, history has not been kind to the native Tejanos, who are still considered "Mexicans" by some Texans. In the early years of the Texas Republic (1836), Texas identity and the Lone Star became inseparable (plate 18). From its inception, the Republic of Texas used the Lone Star to symbolize its independence from Mexico and, paradoxically, its independence from the United States. Historians remind us that the Texas Republic constantly dealt with the issue of sovereignty versus annexation in relation to the United States, and that many Texans anticipated joining the Union from the beginning.[2] Nevertheless, the Texas Republic represented political sovereignty and the star symbolized the isolation and aspirations of Texans (both Texians and Tejanos) who had broken from Mexico.

Thus, the star as a symbol is both political and geographical: political because Texas stood alone, radiant and defiant; geographical because the Texas star symbolizes the expansionist, independent (actually peripheral) location of Texas the country in the context of the world map in the period from 1836 to 1845. It is this period that D. W. Meinig considers crucial to Texas identity. As he puts it: "All interpreters of Texas agree that the ten years of the Republic had an immense psychological impact."[3]

As a visual manifestation of freedom, the star symbolized Republican Texas. In this context, the star is what Alan Gowans calls a substitute image—a picture that serves as substitute for material things and as a symbol for ideas.[4] Gowans reminds us that, "in social function . . . substitute imagery remains the foundation of all traditional artistic activity. High and low arts alike."[5] Gowans is referring to any and all images, such as photographs, art, and maps, that come to stand for the original. Thus, the Lone Star or the Texas map can stand for Texas as an idea and as a place. As didactic or instructional tools, substitute imagery can range from very literal to highly abstract, depending on its use.[6]

A "symbol," as the term is used here and as it is defined by *Webster's International Dictionary*, is "something that stands for or suggests something else by reason of relationship, association, convention or accidental resemblance." The Lone Star is a classic symbol in that it conveys both the state's history and its geographic identity in an abstract form: the star signifies brilliance, isolation, distance, and many other things as an abstract form; through the process of association, these become the qualities we associate with Texas the place.

The Lone Star was incorporated into the official Texas seal on December 10, 1836, when interim president of the Texas Republic David Burnet submitted a design consisting of the star with the letters "The State of Texas" in a circle (fig. 4-1).[7] By the late nineteenth century the star was being used to market a Texas-based service as it was employed in the logo of the Houston & Texas Central Railroad (fig. 4-2). Seen on the sides of boxcars and refrigerator cars, it symbolized Texas to those who saw the railroad's freight cars rolling across the United States. By the 1910s, the star was associated with Texas oil products, as the Texas Company (TEXACO) used it on its distinctive green, black, and silver logo. Since the 1930s, Texaco has made very effective use of the bright red Lone Star as an advertising symbol ("You can trust your car to the man who wears the star"), and many businesses continued the tradition in the 1940s and the 1950s (fig. 4-3).

In some ways, the star was the perfect late nineteenth and early twentieth century logo for Texas. It both conveyed the political status of the state and

FIG. 4-1. The Texas state seal, adopted from David Burnet's 1836 design, features the lone star. Despite the prominence and popularity of the Texas map, the star remains the official symbol of Texas. (Author's collection)

FIG. 4-2. Logo from a 1911 Houston and Texas Central Railroad timetable. The H&TC and its affiliates made effective use of the (lone) star in their logos, called heralds by railroad historians. The boxcars and refrigerator cars of the H&TC served as rolling billboards, reminding people in different parts of the country that Texas was the Lone Star State. This logo is from a 1911 railroad H&TC timetable. (Courtesy DeGolyer Library, Southern Methodist University, Dallas, Texas)

FIG. 4-3. The Lone Star as Texaco's familiar symbol, seen here on a service station sign in Arlington, Texas, has become associated with a Texas product (oil), but it also subconsciously reminds the observer of Texas history and independence. (1994 photo by author)

had a powerful effect on the imagination as astronomy developed into a popular avocation during the era that found millions watching Halley's comet. The star has powerful religious and mythical connotations, and its being stylized to depict a wide range of Texas products would seem nearly inevitable. City directories from the 1910s to the 1950s reveal its popularity as the premier Texas symbol. And yet, the star would seem to have burned brightest up to about the mid 1950s, when other symbols became quite commonly associated with Texas. Today fewer and fewer businesses use the star as their primary identity, while many more are using the Texas map. In fact, many businesses named "Lone Star . . ." have actually adopted the map outline as their logo, relegating the star to a secondary position: Lone Star Trolley of San Antonio is an example (plate 19).

The popular use of the map of Texas seems to have originated with promotion of the state, that is, to get people to Texas around the beginning of the twentieth century. It was used effectively by the Pretorians, whose advertising for a conference in Dallas in 1906 featured an attractive woman pointing to the Texas map, with Dallas indicated by a star. The railroads were especially adept at using the map for promotion. An early use of the map (1909) finds it serving as the target for an arrow that symbolizes the southwestward thrusting Iron Mountain railroad lines (fig. 4-4). Interestingly, the map of Texas is stylized and not particularly accurate in shape, yet it serves the purpose of illustrating destination: Texas.

Despite its early use as embellishment on promotional material, the map of Texas did not actually appear on a railroad logo until the 1950s, when the Texas-Mexican Railway adopted the map and a star to symbolize its service area (fig. 4-5). Today this attractive orange and yellow logo appears on the locomotives, freight cars, and even the service vehicles of the Texas-Mexican. Interestingly, this railroad with connections south of the border does not feature a map of Mexico; rather, the state of Texas and the Lone Star— which serves to imply the compasslike orientation of the railroad's service— reinforce the Texas orientation of the Laredo-based railroad. It should come as no surprise that two newly created Texas regional short line railroads, the Chaparral and the Texas NorthEastern, use the map in their logos. The Texas NorthEastern's logo dates from the 1980s and, significantly, includes only the map and the company's name, rather than the star (fig. 4-6).

The relationship between star and the map has been an intimate one for more than fifty years. As we have seen, they seem to work well together as design elements that emphasize the expansive, radiant aspects of Texas. As the map identity has become stronger, we now occasionally see the Texas map outline actually substituting for (that is, replacing) the Lone Star in some clever versions of the Texas flag (such as the Texas tourism bumper sticker) or, quite commonly, the rectangular shape of the Texas flag replaced by the Texas map outline so that the map itself actually becomes a flag (plate 20).

FIG. 4-4. This Texas map appeared as a detail on a 1909 railroad route map and offers an embryonic glimpse of the Texas map's popularity. The design, which incorporates a chain-link arrow symbolizing the directness of the railroad's connections, serves as a caricature of the state's shape by eliminating the western tip near El Paso. It was produced by the Poole Brothers of Chicago. (Courtesy Special Collections Division, University of Texas at Arlington Libraries)

FIG. 4-5. The logo of the Texas-Mexican Railway features a map and the Texas star—a common combination of images. Developed in the 1950s, this appears to be the first railroad herald to feature a Texas map. (Author's collection)

FIG. 4-6. The logo of the Texas North-Eastern Railroad, a regional shortline created during the deregulation era of the 1980s, features a Texas map. (Courtesy Texas NorthEastern Railroad)

One of the more striking, and novel, uses of the map on a flag is seen on the newscasts of KMOL in San Antonio (fig. 4-7), where the map of Texas forms the top of a red, white, and blue banner that is seen to the right side of the newscasters. According to station manager Bob Donahue, this icon represents a compromise that symbolizes the importance of Texas and recognizes the strong patriotism of the troops at nearby military installations such as Fort Sam Houston and Lackland Air Force Base. In this context, the map of Texas stands for state and national patriotism.

Rather than being iconoclastic (that is, a renunciation of the Lone Star), these modifications to the Texas flag appear to confirm, and perhaps to further encourage, Texans' nearly legendary pride in their state. Whereas the Lone Star is a highly abstract image that connotes independence, the map outline of Texas is a tangible symbol of place. Unlike the star, the map is never confused with any other symbol; thus, it is now probably more functional than the Lone Star image in advertising Texas. In other words, the map is both a symbol *and* an icon (that is, a pictorial representation or image), and therefore it is capable of conveying visual as well as metaphorical information about Texas the place. In a very real and paradoxical way, then, we may consider the map (to paraphrase Gowans' terminology) a substitute image that communicates information on several levels simultaneously.

Studying Tex-map mania can help us understand more about the state's changing identity—which may actually embody as well as transcend national identity. Many Texans consider themselves residents of a foreign country (Texas) as well as residents of a nation (the United States). I am reminded of the time demonstrators at an international rally in Washington, D.C., were asked to march in separate columns—one for the states and one for other countries; the Texas-flag-bearing contingent immediately walked over to the international section! To Texans, the tourism industry's claim, "Texas—it's a whole other country"[8] is more than a clever slogan; it is also rooted in perceptions of the state as a separate geopolitical entity. Texas "passports" are a popular item in gift shops. Spurious in their authority, they jokingly remind us that Texas is/was another country. Significantly, they feature several "official" Texas symbols on their pages, including silhouette images of the Lone Star, longhorn cattle, and (naturally) the map of Texas (fig. 4-8). In the 1950s, fake Texas money (in the form of U.S. paper currency) was produced; it, too, featured a map of Texas on one corner of the bill, perhaps a reminder that Texas did produce its own currency during the Republican period, when, paradoxically, no such map existed.

Texas has come to signify "national" identity—in the vernacular at least. For example, I saw a Louisiana Pacific load of lumber stamped with "Made in U.S.A.," but the outline it appeared on was a map of Texas (plate 21). This may seem perplexing or even chauvinistic to non-Texans. After all, one might ask, how can Texas be confused with being America when it is simply

FIG. 4-7. Assuming the dominant position once reserved for the star in Texas iconography, the Texas map is featured in this powerful red, white, and blue graphic that flanks the newscasters on television station KMOL in San Antonio. (Photo courtesy KMOL TV)

FIG. 4-8. Iconography on the Official Texas Passport features a Texas map. Although a gag item, these passports designed by Bill Collins are reminders of Texas' claim to independence—a claim that remains unrelinquished in the popular ideology. (Photo by author)

one part of the country? After many discussions with Texans, I conclude that Texas is also a metaphor for American nationalism, for Texas epitomizes American values. Texans are not simply "patriotic" about being Americans; many consider their state's history to be quintessentially American—more American than America's. Therefore, they see no inconsistency in using a map of Texas to symbolize the United States, for, in some ways, Texas is what the rest of the country ought to be—the best (read "only") place in the world to live. This is a subtle way of verifying the principle that the United States is a series of independent states, the most independent (i.e., republican) having been Texas.

Texas, which is rooted in a brief but romanticized republican past, offers a geographic identity that is unique in the history of the United States. In other words, the power of "imperial Texas," as D. W. Meinig identified it, is still an operative memory. Texans will always remind visitors and newcomers that they stood alone in their fight for independence and, when they did so, they held a sprawling frontier empire peripheral to both the United States and Mexico. Virtually every Texan can list the six countries whose flags have flown over the state. When the popular Six Flags Over Texas theme park was first developed, its name was intended to be "Texas under Six Flags" until a board member proclaimed that "Texas has never been *under* anything!"[9] The state map helped Texans reaffirm a historical and mystical independent sense of place and pride as their state became more and more international in its orientation during the 1950s and the 1960s.

In the late twentieth century, Tex-map mania helps us understand that a map serves many purposes, and in its most elementary form—the outline or silhouette—it may become an icon or symbol of identity. When a geographic outline is truly distinctive and can substitute for other, more abstract, symbols, it can effectively symbolize history, identity, and attachment to place. Consider Bill DeOre's cartoon in the *Dallas Morning News* dealing with the relocation of one of Texas' premier industries of the last two decades— L.T.V.—to Cleveland. DeOre symbolized L.T.V.'s removal by depicting the Texas-shaped root system of a Cleveland-bound tree (fig. 4-9). Interestingly, the map of Texas is correctly proportioned and oriented, but would have left a reverse image of Texas as it was pulled out of the ground. As we have seen, though, that image would still have been recognizable.

The process by which the Texas map became a symbol for Texas (and "southwestern") identity tells us much about the way Texas and the region have been viewed by Texans and non-Texans. As a territorial or spatial symbol, one would assume that the Texas map would appear on the earliest form of graphic identification—the cattle brand. After all, we have seen that a car dealer effectively used a Texas-shaped cattle brand in advertising. Certainly, the association between Texas and cattle reinforces the state's expansive "Wild West" image. The Texas map is used in about forty registered

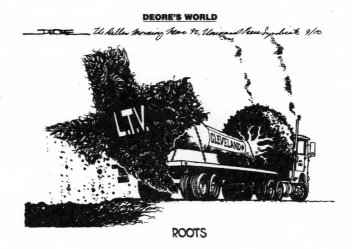

FIG. 4-9. In this classic cartoon by Bill DeOre in the September 10, 1992, issue of the *Dallas Morning News,* L.T.V.'s announced plan to leave Texas for Cleveland, Ohio, is seen as an uprooting, wrenching experience. (Courtesy *Dallas Morning News*)

cattle brands, most of which are quite recent. In fact, the curator of the Texas Cattleman's Museum in Fort Worth could not trace any Texas-shaped brand before the 1930s.[10]

Two factors prevented the map's being used as a brand in the nineteenth century. The first is technical: the shape of Texas is very complicated and the numerous bends and angles encourage too much heat to build up, which can damage the hide and produce an irregular "burn." The second is perceptual: the map of Texas simply was not thought of as a symbol in the nineteenth century. Ranchers were identifying their spreads with brands, and few included "Texas" in ranch names. Besides, the image of Texas as a geographic territory was probably vaguer at that time and was symbolized effectively by the Lone Star. This confirms my general observation that the use of the Texas map to symbolize "Texas" is a relatively recent phenomenon.

How far back can we trace the map as an advertising symbol? Study of city directories, which are found as early as the mid-nineteenth century, reveals that the map was not employed as a symbol before the turn of the century, and began to appear more often in the 1910s. At first, Texas maps were used to convey location and direction, or to depict Texas in relation to other states. With the development of clever graphics like the Iron Mountain Railway cartogram seen earlier (fig. 4-4), serious mapmakers began to use Texas maps to convey additional information about the state. Maps became more than mere maps in the hands of experienced mapmakers; by the teens and the twenties they had become pictographic caricatures of places, and Texas began to develop its characteristic (if not stereotypic) image at about this time. This probably coincided with the popularity of the animated cartoon in movie theaters.

Rogers' Fort Worth official map in Morrison and Fourmy's Fort Worth

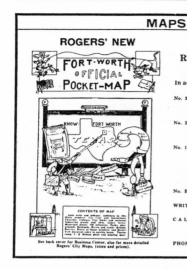

FIG. 4-10. This 1925 map does far more than simply orient the observer; it conveys information in a whimsical fashion similar to the cartoons that became quite popular in movie theaters at the time. (Courtesy Special Collections Division, The University of Texas at Arlington Libraries)

City Directory of 1925 (fig. 4-10) provides a good example, for it serves to do more than simply orient the reader. In this advertisement, the outline of Texas is combined with slogans and other graphics. Significantly, the Texas map is depicted on a billboard, which implies that people would see it from the road. Although this is not the earliest of the Texas map outlines, its development by a mapmaker and its depiction in an automobile-oriented format is significant. Texas map symbolism would soon flourish, apparently a product of the automobile age in which, for the first time, the public began to navigate using road maps. If the automobile increased our need for maps, it also provided an incentive (and increased the public's appetite) for map-styled graphics. What may have begun with promotional imagery by the railroads flowered in the automobile era.

By the early 1930s, stylized Texas maps became more common. Consider, for example, the Pearl beer advertisement from a 1933 issue of the *Southwestern Railway Journal*, a union publication for the region's railroaders. The company used a prophetic advertising statement ("What Texas Makes Makes Texas") and depicted Pearl beer as the "Thirst Choice of Taste-Wise Texans" (fig. 4-11). To convey the Texas loyalty and pride theme, this advertisement uses an obliquely positioned map on which stands a tall (and presumably cold) glass of beer. Significantly, the map features a series of sunburst lines, which help convey a sense of brilliance and radiance. The message is unmistakable: Pearl beer is a product that emanates from the Lone Star State. In the 1930s, Pearl beer used the Texas map to identify its product in a wide variety of publications. One ad that would not be acceptable today shows Santa Claus holding a bottle of Pearl lager beer; a Texas map is used in a wreath, demonstrating how beautifully the map fits into a circular format

FIG. 4-11. A 1933 Pearl Beer advertisement conveys action by using an oblique outline map out of which lines radiate—and reminds us that the Texas map has been used as a powerful symbol in advertising for over half a century. (Courtesy Special Collections Division, The University of Texas at Arlington Libraries)

FIG. 4-12. In a 1938 Pearl Beer advertisement in the *San Antonio Express*, Santa Claus enjoys a bottle of lager beer, and a Texas map appears in a circular wreath. (Courtesy *San Antonio Express*)

(fig. 4-12). This use of a wreath is reminiscent of the state seal and the Texas Historical Commission's seal: both give Texas an auspicious if not ancient Roman/European association, graphically speaking.

By the Texas centennial in 1936, the Texas map had become a stylized symbol for automotive mobility, as seen in a fascinating oblique map that urges, "Texans! Plan to Travel Texas during—Centennial Year" and features four automobiles rushing toward each other from the cardinal directions (fig. 4-13).

Newspaper advertisements of the later 1930s—especially those in San Antonio—featured an array of interesting Texas map images. Consider, for example, two from the *San Antonio Express*. The first (fig. 4-14) is partly informational in that it depicts the geographic relationship between San Antonio and Laredo in advertising the "gateway into Mexico" location of the latter. Note the bold letters of the word "Laredo" stretched across the map, accompanied by the slogan. The graphics themselves, as well as the message, urge action. Clearly, such maps are linked to the mobility that became possible in the automobile era.

In another advertisement (fig. 4-15), the Brannon-Signaigo Cigar Company proclaimed that Lovera Cigars (which had been "a Texas 10¢ favorite for over 25 years") were now 5 cents. The company used the map to advertise a cigar with the slogan, "In Tyler, Palestine and all points west . . . Texas smokers want mildness and fragrant aroma."

Significantly, even at this early date, advertisers used two techniques in Texas map-based advertising that are still common: (1) partial obscuring or covering of the map with other advertising symbols—in the Lovera case, figures of men smoking cigars and a box of cigars; and (2) the familiar relief shading of the southern, eastern, or western border of Texas to give the map image a sense of solidity, one might say, to reaffirm Texas as "topography," or, more to the point, as a geographic place.

These advertisements confirm that Texas maps have been used to convey a sense of location, association, and action for more than half a century. They are meant to stimulate and motivate as well as to inform the map reader. Although we could trace Texas map designs for the sixty-year period between 1930 and 1990 and perhaps find some subtle design changes, we must be impressed by the design continuity and the persistent use of cartographic techniques such as the outline and the silhouette. Consider the continuity between the Lovera cigar ad and a May, 1992, advertisement announcing "The Return of the Chili Queens"—a Tex-Mex *conjunto* band (fig. 4-16). This ad features an accordion stretched open (that is, presumably playing) and the words "Cerveza Lite" across the map. In both maps we can see the tendency to overlay themes of action (often horizontally oriented) across the map of Texas. After researching the history of Texas maps used in advertising, I believe that they have become a bit more sophisticated and

FIG. 4-13. This design format, which appeared in the March, 1936, issue of the *Southwestern Railway Journal,* features an obliquely viewed Texas map in relief. It beautifully depicts centripetal motion on the expansive, centrifugal outline of Texas. (Courtesy Special Collections Division, The University of Texas at Arlington Libraries)

FIG. 4-14. The state map commonly helps identify particular geographic locations and makes a point about them. Here, in a 1938 advertisement from the *San Antonio Express,* Laredo (marked by a star) is shown in relation to San Antonio (a black dot). The designer has used the congruent shape of the Panhandle to feature "L" in Laredo. (Courtesy *San Antonio Express*)

FIG. 4-15. In this 1938 advertisement for Lovera Cigars in the *San Antonio Express,* an oblique Texas map becomes the stage upon which action is depicted: smokers enjoying cigars across the state. (Courtesy *San Antonio Express*)

FIG. 4-16. A 1992 flyer uses a Texas map and an accordion to advertise Hispanic *conjunto* bands. (Author's collection)

technically better reproduced, but they still rely on certain important design assumptions and traditions.

This Miller Lite beer advertisement reminds us that the map of Texas has important cultural as well as commercial associations. It is commonly seen in Spanish-language advertising, which confirms that the Texas map has been adopted by Hispanic culture—a situation that is also demonstrated by the use of the map as a logo for the 1991 *conjunto* cassette by Tierra Tejana, a Hispanic pop band.

That the map of Texas, which appears to have first been popularized by Anglo American commercial advertisers, is now adopted by Texans of diverse backgrounds is apparent in a flyer announcing a November, 1992, "Chicano Empowerment in Texas" conference (fig. 4-17). The pictorial/graphic information within the outline map of Texas features several images of Hispanic peoples and icons, as well as signs featuring the words "La Raza," "Chicano Huelga" [Strike], "Libertad" [Liberty], and "Poder" [Power]. The National Association of Chicano Scholars designed the conference to address many issues, including the "diversity and uniqueness of Mexicanos and Latinos," which have "been conflated into an easily appropriated identity by liberal discourses that feign respect and interest."[11] The map of Texas can excite our passion for independence and territory, and its use in this Hispanic context is particularly effective and instructive—especially in light of Terry Jordan's

FIG. 4-17. In this 1992 flyer for a Chicano conference, Hispanic identity is conveyed by a series of powerful photographic images within the map of Texas. Once highly associated with Anglo power, the map of Texas had become an important symbol of ethnic solidarity for some groups by the 1980s. (Author's collection)

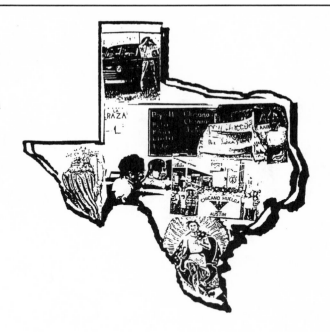

FIG. 4-18. Two important symbols—the map of Texas and the Irish clover—are used on this bumper sticker to identify an Irish-Texan driver. (Photo by author)

claim that the growing power of Latino peoples in Texas has helped renew and intensify a sense of Anglo Texan homeland identity.[12]

The Texas map also serves to identify other ethnic groups, such as German, Polish, Czech, and Irish Texans. A bumper sticker (fig. 4-18) incorporating two symbols—the clover and the Texas map—mixes metaphors and cultural identities, but it has the effect of unifying a people (the Irish/Irish Americans) and a place (Texas). Similarly, the menu for Picha's Czech American Restaurant in West, Texas, features a Czech flag in the form of a Texas map (fig. 4-19).

These groups have clearly assimilated in that they are white Euro-Ameri-

FIG. 4-19. The menu for this ethnic restaurant in the town of West, Texas, features a hand-drawn map outline with a stylized Czech flag. (Author's collection)

cans. Although African-American identity is occasionally linked with the Texas map, African Americans most often use the outline or silhouette map of Africa (which is a powerful symbol implying "continental" as well as "exotic" geography). The persistence of the map of Africa in this regard is quite interesting. It may symbolize the African roots of all African Americans, or it may correspond to a rise in black nationalism and separatism. The map of Africa eclipses the Texas map in African-American graphic designs in the Lone Star State, where blacks were denied knowledge of the Union victory in the Civil War until June of the following year—hence, the annual Juneteenth celebration of emancipation. Once again, maps may tell us as much as, or more than, rhetoric does.

To continue with our historical analysis of the Texas map, we need to ask when it first became an exported—that is, a national or international—graphic design. My research confirms the widespread use of the Texas map beginning in the mid 1930s—more specifically 1936. According to Jim Steely of the Texas Historical Commission,[13] the state outline map appears to have been used first as an official border marker ("Welcome to Texas") during the 1936 Texas Centennial (fig. 4-20). Slightly modified and somewhat art deco in design, the shape of Texas accommodates the large letters T-E-X-A-S. Fragile corners are rounded, and the stone base solidly supports the masonry map image. Thus, visitors to the state came to recognize the map as synonymous with Texas. There is considerable continuity here, too, as bold silhouette maps are often used because they can be recognized by motorists moving at high speeds. Today one sees many official uses of the outline, from a subtle

FIG. 4-20. In the 1930s the State Highway Department began placing the now familiar signs welcoming visitors to Texas. This drawing provides specifications for a marker near Amarillo. (Courtesy Craig A. Steffens, Texas Department of Transportation, and Jim Steely, Texas Historical Commission)

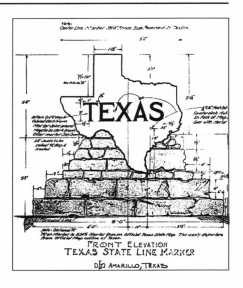

background image on car titles, to a sobering outline for the numerous "DWI—You Can't Afford It" signs alongside roads and highways (fig. 4-21), but they seem to derive from the 1930s markers.

The earliest use of the Texas map in advertising a product marketed outside of Texas appears to be the Liquid Sunshine citrus drink marketed by Lazenby of the Dr Pepper Company in Waco, circa 1936.[14] The bottle depicted a map inside the shape of a grapefruit—a juxtaposition that reminds us once again of the symmetry of the Texas map and its ability to fit into a circle (fig. 4-22).

Since the 1930s, the map of Texas has found its way into postcards, logos, and gift shop kitsch such as shot glasses. By the early 1950s, Texas-shaped signs were used in highway and main street advertising, for example, on a sign for the Arlington State Bank (fig. 4-23). Although a watershed was reached when Texas Instruments began using its Texas map logo internationally after 1952, Texas map usage continued to increase within the state and across the nation. We can still find Eisenhower for President buttons featuring only a Texas map and the word "Ike" (fig. 4-24). Moviegoing audiences across the country experienced the Texas map in an intriguing poster for *The Lady from Texas,* a 1951 western ranching drama from Universal-International Pictures, the locale of which was verified by a distorted but nevertheless recognizable map of Texas (plate 22). The map is also seen on a wall behind the actors in the 1962 version of *State Fair,* a film that conveys an image of Texas as a piece of western, rural America.

A wide variety of Texas maps were used through the 1960s and the 1970s on an array of merchandise and logos. By 1980, innumerable Texas map–

FIG. 4-21. These DWI (Driving While Intoxicated) signs, which became a common sight on Texas highways in the early 1990s, not only presented driving sober as an official value but emphasized the penalties for the offense. (1993 photo by author)

FIG. 4-22. Lazenby's Liquid Sunshine was a citrus drink marketed in the mid-1930s by the Dr Pepper Company. On this amber-colored bottle, the map of Texas is superimposed on a yellow grapefruit. The tip and Panhandle protrude slightly, giving the graphic an even more expansive quality. (Photo by author; courtesy Dr Pepper Museum, Waco, Texas)

FIG. 4-23. When erected in February, 1953, Arlington State Bank's Texas-shaped sign captured the attention of the local newspaper, whose photographer recorded bank officials admiring the new sign. (Courtesy *Arlington Citizen Journal* and Special Collections Division, University of Texas at Arlington Libraries)

FIG. 4-24. By the 1950s, the Texas map had become familiar on numerous kitsch items and lapel pins. Here only a single name and the map imply local endorsement of native son Dwight D. Eisenhower in 1956. (Author's collection)

shaped items could be found. They had become even more commonplace by the Texas Sesquicentennial in 1986, when *Esprit, The Magazine of the Mid-Cities* could illustrate "Deep in the Shape of Texas," a panoply of products shaped like the state. The map's use continues to the present. Certainly, Tex-map mania is strongly associated with commerce and trade—especially services, food, and leisure products.

Visitors to Texas are often struck by the proliferation of Texas maps, and few Texas maps are more memorable than those in neon (plate 23). As if to accentuate the state's radiance and energy, neon signs for a wide range of products and services (especially beer) light the night—or the dark interiors of bars and nightspots. Once again, we see technology affecting cartography. Because neon tubes are limited by the tightness of curves, they produce maps that are somewhat abstract and simplified; not every curve of the Red River or the Rio Grande can be reproduced. But that illustrates the beauty of neon in simplifying the complex and creating an integrated composition (fig. 4-25). Neon signs remind us that the Texas map is omnipresent in the exterior landscape and in interior merchandising. They also remind us that designers are constantly searching for the most effective techniques to portray the map image of the state.

Many Texans immersed in the map fad report being "so used to seeing the map" that they are surprised to learn that the Texas map as icon is a relatively recent (i.e., a mid-to-late-twentieth-century) phenomenon. If personal mobility helped popularize the map in the first place, continued mobility is reinforcing its popular use. Texans are increasingly aware that their huge state is shrinking as a consequence of improved highways and commuter airlines. As fewer and fewer Texans can claim to be native born, and American popular culture sweeps not only the country but the world, the map serves to reaffirm Texas as a unique place with historical and geographical roots.

Regarding such perceptual and geographic issues, we must ask if the Texas map is seen everywhere in Texas, or only in certain locations. Intensive fieldwork reveals that the map is seen throughout the state, but that it is seen more frequently in some parts or regions of Texas than in others. Although the Texas map is nearly ubiquitous, a detailed study of the Yellow Pages across the state suggests that it is used most heavily in tourist-conscious San Antonio and in metropolitan Northeast Texas. David Filewood's study of the Yellow Pages in twenty Texas communities suggests that the map is most commonly used in Central and East Texas;[15] Austin would appear to be the center perceptually as well as politically, with the Rio Grande Valley, San Antonio, and Fort Worth–Dallas being quite Texas map-oriented. Conversely, El Paso, Galveston, and Nacogdoches—all located at the borders of the state—appear to use the map somewhat less frequently than the norm. This was confirmed by field checking of billboards and local signs in 1991–92.

Nevertheless, the map can be said to be ubiquitous. Despite a growing sense of vernacular regionalism on the part of Texans who may also consider themselves residents of the "Hill Country," "West Texas," "the Metroplex," or the "Heart of Texas" (plate 24),[16] then, the Texas map reinforces attachment to Texas as home. We see the Texas map symbol in urban, suburban, and rural settings—in all of the state's cultural regions from border to border. Therefore, we should not be surprised to find it in rural areas, where it may be seen on a ranch gateway (plate 25), or in the state's many towns, as well as on high-rise buildings in the state's metropolitan areas such as Houston, San Antonio, Dallas, and Fort Worth (fig. 4-26).

The Texas map appears to be commonly associated with an aggressive, proud, Anglo Texan population that is promoting products and services; but, as noted earlier, it is finding its way into "ethnic" advertising—a sure sign of its widespread acceptance. From available data, we may conclude

FIG. 4-25. Neon signs, like this one for a shoe repair shop in Arlington, use a simplified outline of the Texas map together with some appropriate symbol to promote their stores. Here, the word *shoe* remained unilluminated as its owner awaited the funds to repair it. (1992 photo by author)

FIG. 4-26. Urban Texas: Set into a façade of pink granite and reflected by the Texas sky, a brass map of Texas helps to identify the Texas Building in downtown Fort Worth. (1992 photo by author)

that Tex-map mania began as an urban advertising phenomenon, and there is some indication that non-Texans in places like Chicago and New York may have been advocates of its early use in Texas advertising. It was certainly used by Texans during the middle years of the twentieth century as leaders in both the private and the public sectors seized on it to convey a sense of Texas identity. Today it permeates virtually all aspects of Texas society and economy. It symbolizes Texas and Texas products at a time when geographic identity is important in establishing a world market for products; thus, it might be said to be a perfect geographic manifestation of materialism. But the map has even deeper meaning than that.

The Map of Texas and "Spiritual" Symbolism

That the Texas map is widely used on ephemeral as well as durable items, and on frivolous as well as serious items, reveals its broad appeal. We must conclude that the map fad serves many purposes when we find the Texas map on T-shirts, license plates, and historical markers. The most serious— and permanent—use of the Texas map, it would seem, is also the most ultimately place-oriented: as grave markers in Texas cemeteries. Where else but in Texas could one find gravestones in the shape of the deceased's state? Surely, the Texas-shaped monuments or markers that one occasionally sees in cemeteries (fig. 4-27) epitomize a person's attachment to place. Darwin Spearing, in *Roadside Geology of Texas,* calls Texas-shaped granite headstones "Pure Texas."[17] Here the use of two symbols—stone for eternity, the Texas map for history and geography—reinforces the uniqueness of the Texan spirit. According to Texas monument dealer Ron Henry, these stones are occasionally made out of pink Texas granite but—ironically—they are often quarried and cut by Vermont or other northeastern stonecutters to the specifications of Texas dealers. The biographical information, and occasionally an epitaph, are added by local monument dealers.[18]

It is fitting that we can find the Texas map in the cemetery, where the cycle of life is completed, for the Texas map serves to reaffirm attachment to place— much as it does on the AIDS memorial quilt mentioned in chapter 2. Although epitaphs may often stress that the person has left this earth for heaven, we should not be surprised to find Texas as an icon. If, as we have seen, some Texans consider the state about as close as one can get to heaven, then the appearance of the map on their tombstones is predictable. Whether Texans making references to their state as heaven are overly enthusiastic, or understandably defensive, remains a moot point. Tanya Tucker's popular song, "Texas When I Die," states that "when I die I may not go to heaven, 'cause I don't know if they let cowboys in. If they don't, just let me go to Texas, 'cause Texas is as close as I've been." Although Texas was portrayed as paradise by promoters as early as the 1830s, we should remember that General Phil Sheridan was reported to have opined—after a hot trip from San

FIG. 4-27. Texas-shaped gravestones, seen in some of the state's cemeteries, symbolize a deep loyalty. This one in Galveston was photographed on a monument dealer's lot. (1992 photo by Herb Weisberg)

Antonio to Galveston in August, 1866—"If I owned Texas and Hell, I would rent out Texas and live in Hell." Non-Texans may be amused or bewildered by the Texan's fierce attachment to place that results in a Texas-shaped gravestone, but loyalty to Texas and Texas map usage go hand in hand. Both know very few limits. A Texas-shaped gravestone, then, seems a fitting artifact to symbolize a life spent in a place that is as much a state of mind as a state of the union.

The Texas map is used to celebrate Christmas, for it is seen in displays of colored lights secured to metal rods that have been twisted into the shape of Texas (plate 26). The visitor to Texas may be bewildered by the juxtaposition of Texas maps and the slogan "Merry Christmas, Y'all" in Christmas lights, but to the Texan, it is simply a matter of true reverence for both the holiday and the state. Texas, as noted earlier, commands a sense of patriotism and devotion, and Texans are proud of that fact.

The ultimate spiritual use of the map of Texas is seen in the musical pageants at Fiesta Texas in San Antonio. This theme park, which opened in 1992, is worthy of much comment, for it depicts or reenacts Texas history in several areas, such as Los Festivales (the Mexican town where a fiesta is always in progress), Spassburg (a German Texas community where it is always Oktoberfest), and Crackaxle Canyon (a ca. 1920 boom town anticipating the arrival of President Coolidge). Visitors to Fiesta Texas have an entertaining and educational experience that builds on the history of Texas.

At Fiesta Texas, the park's early visitors also experienced "The Heart of Texas," a musical odyssey that began with the state's Mexican heritage, moved through the battle of the Alamo, and concluded with modern Texas. As the musical concluded with a medley of popular songs about Texas, a huge map filled the stage. During the songs, the map was transformed from a bold, black silhouette surrounded by red light to a dazzling outline rimmed by two rows of white incandescent lights (plate 27). During the songs, a flag of the United States as wide as the stage was brought down over the map of Texas. Significantly, the lights outlining Texas' perimeter still shone through this translucent U.S. flag. At the conclusion of the show, the U.S. flag was lifted and the Texas map outline once again dominated the stage. The Texas map was illuminated until the last viewer left the auditorium. The audience left with a powerful message that loyalty to Texas is inseparable from American patriotism. Fiesta Texas continues to use this illuminated map for other musical shows about the Lone Star State.

In this context, the map reaffirms a commitment to Texas and American political beliefs (independence, democracy, loyalty, and so on), but watching such musical shows makes one aware that Texas identity and patriotism go beyond politics and enter the realm of religious, or at any rate, deeply spiritual, experience. In these pageants, the map of Texas blazes as a symbol of resurrection following martyrdom at the Alamo (and Goliad), reminding the audience that, like Christianity, Texas independence involved the ultimate sacrifice. In this context, the map is a superb symbol, for it conjures up not only a Lone Star identity but also the iconography of both the star and the cross. Voices rise to a crescendo, the musical concludes, and the audience rises to its feet as the singers exit the stage and, significantly, only the map outline of Texas remains illuminated as the audience makes its way out of the theater.

Pageants such as "The Heart of Texas" at Fiesta Texas represent the ultimate in Texas iconography. They bring together images of Hispanic, Anglo pioneer, frontier culture; oil, cattle, and aerospace; rural and urban imagery. Their songs unite the two major cultures presented at the theme park (Anglo and Hispanic), and all of these images culminate in the most recent symbol or icon for Texas identity: the Texas map.

The powerful and easily identified map of Texas makes a perfect, noncontroversial, secular symbol, but it is also a powerful spiritual symbol; its stellar and cruciform shape conveys the power of birth, martyrdom, and resurrection. It simultaneously (and subtly) reminds us of Texas' political and historical aspirations, and the powerful unifying "Christian" symbolism of the two dominant Texas religions (Catholicism and Protestantism) under Mexican and Anglo American rule. By association, it also conveys the size and energy of Texas.

Because it is capable of conveying so many powerful messages, the Texas map is both symbolic and iconographic. On one level it simply stands for Texas; but on other, deeper levels, it also symbolizes the values—such as independence, loyalty, and sacrifice—that remain a part of the mystique of Texas identity to Texans and the world.

Epilogue:
The Map of Texas and the Future

THE TEXAS MAP SEEMS TO HAVE GAINED SUCH CURRENCY THAT COCA COLA billboards seen in 1994 feature only the distinctive outline of a Coke bottle with the slogan "the Shape of Texas." This assumes that the reader will draw an abstract conclusion, linking the shape of Texas not only with the map but with the shape of their product's package or container. Similarly, the map is so ingrained in popular culture that students in Bedford sent to collect old editions of the Yellow Pages for recycling in July, 1994, created what the newspapers called "The Yellow Rows of Texas"—a huge pile of the phone books in, as the reader might guess, the shape of the Texas map.[1] It is significant that the first widely marketed "holusion" (holographic illusion) image poster marketed by N Vision Grafix of Las Colinas was a Texas map that materialized after the reader stared at what appeared to be only a field of bluebonnets. This revolutionary computer-generated art form was pioneered by Texans Michael Bielinski and Paul Herber and was featured in the March, 1994, issue of *Texas Monthly*. Their first poster has been marketed nationally and internationally—helping to spread the image of the Texas map to all corners of the globe.

Time will tell whether the Texas map will continue to become even more popular, or become so common that it will lose its impact after saturating the market. (It is interesting to note that 1991 plans for the Ballpark or stadium in Arlington called for Texas maps to be among the icons, but that when this magnificent stadium opened in April of 1994, it featured only more traditional Texas icons—the Lone Star and longhorns—as embellishments of its spectacular façades.) For the time being, however, the map is still the most popular and effective icon for Texas identity, for, as we have seen, it reminds viewers of both the state's geography and its history.

The map helps orient people to Texas as a place as well as an idea. In this sense, it is not surprising that the map has become the dominant symbol of Texas at exactly the time when place is an important commodity marketed by image makers who are concerned with establishing international trade connections. In this regard, Texas' supranational identity is an asset, for the recent passage of the North American Free Trade Agreement (NAFTA) is expected to diminish the importance of national borders while benefiting enterprising states, such as Texas, which are located proximate to the border. Significantly, too, the Texas map helps Texans identify with the state at a time when it is growing rapidly and many proudly lay claim to being native Texans. In reality, the map helps generate a sense of belonging in all Texans, newcomers and natives alike. It reminds us that one of Texas' greatest traditions (under Mexican as well as Anglo rule) has been the encouragement of growth by immigration. Both Texas' "friendly" image, as well as its actual economy, have been important factors in encouraging growth. Texas has become the second most populous state in the late twentieth century, meaning that only one state map, California's, can mean "home" to more people.

Viewed in the context of popular culture, the map of Texas is a stabilizing, conservative influence in that it serves as a reminder of the state's traditions at a time when the state is more cosmopolitan than ever. Ironically, at a time when Texas could be overwhelmed by trends in popular culture that tend to make places across the country (and around the world, for that matter) more similar, Texans are using the very dynamic processes of popular culture (advertising and the media) to ensure a sense of Texas identity.[2] Thus, although the popular use of the map of Texas has its roots in promotional efforts beginning almost a century ago (and beginning to flourish half a century ago), it is part of an ongoing process of geographic image building.

That, in essence, is what the phenomenon of Tex-map mania is about—the creation of an image of place. Through the symbolic and iconic use of maps, old images of Texas are reinforced and new ones created. These images not only are marketed by commercial enterprises, they also are found at the heart of Texas' identity in vernacular culture. Maps of this type become part of the language of culture because they are linked to the processes of cultural identity. This study confirms the flexibility of maps as part of the systems by which a culture defines itself: through associative imagery, maps are able to convey cultural traditions (for example, Texas as the sprawling Wild West of the cowboy), and through multicultural imagery, cultural change (Texas as home to diverse cultures). Whereas some critics may interpret the dominance of the map as an indicator of Texans' xenophobia, the reader is urged to view it more sympathetically—as a reflection of a multifaceted pride in the state's culture, history, and geography. Viewed in this manner, the map of Texas transcends the informational role we normally associate with maps and becomes part of the symbolic content of the visual and narrative languages people use to describe—and even to create—places.

Notes

Introduction

1. Leonard Sanders, *How Fort Worth Became the Texas Most City.*
2. Richard Francaviglia, "Tex-Map Mania: The Outline of Texas As a Popular Symbol," *Journal of Cultural Geography* 12, no. 1 (fall\winter, 1991): 69–77.
3. "Girlfriend Finds His Idea of a Ring Isn't Very Engaging," *The Dallas Morning News*, May 14, 1994, sect. C, p. 2.
4. Ibid.

1. Maps and Identity

1. J. B. Harley, "Text and Contexts in the Interpretation of Early Maps," pp. 3–15.
2. Thom Marshall, "Stately Shape Y'all Know," *Houston Chronicle*, Aug. 16, 1992, p. 2.
3. Mark Monomier and George Schnell, *Map Appreciation*, p. 354.
4. Terry G. Jordan, with John L. Bean Jr. and William M. Holmes, *Texas: A Geography*, pp. 269–81.
5. Don Graham, "Texas Videos," *Texas Monthly*, July, 1991, pp. 100–101.
6. John Mills, interview with author, Arlington, Texas, Nov. 3, 1992.

2. The Shape of Texas

1. "Horse of a Different Color," *Austin American Statesman*, May 26, 1993, sect. B, p. 2.
2. Mary Harbit Hecox, telephone conversation with author, July 5, 1994.
3. Marshall, "Stately Shape Y'all Know," p. 1.
4. Ibid.
5. Jim Steely, letter/report to author, April 19, 1994.
6. David Filewood, Yellow Pages survey, University of Texas at Arlington, unpublished research project, Sept., 1992.
7. Yi Fu Tuan, "Language and the Making of Place: A Narrative-Descriptive Approach," *Annals of the Association of American Geographers* 81, no. 4 (Dec., 1991): 685.
8. Dennis Reinhartz, "Greetings from the Lone Star State: Postcard, Cartoon, and Souvenir Maps of Texas," *The Map Collector* (spring, 1993).

9. Richard Meyer, note to the author, Dec. 12, 1993. Meyer is a folklorist and an authority in the symbolism of thanatology.

10. Maryln Schwartz, "Feelings Go Deep for the Great State," *Dallas Morning News,* Oct. 15, 1991, sec. C, p. 1.

11. Michael Kashgarian, "Garden Was a Tribute to Texas—Late Midlander Wiley W. Walls Planted Hundreds of Chinese Elms in the Shape of the Lone Star State," *Midland Reporter-Telegram,* Oct. 17, 1993, sect. C, pp. 2, 3.

3. The Creation of an Icon

1. See Robert S. Martin and James C. Martin, *Contours of Discovery: Printed Maps Delineating the Texas and Southwestern Chapters in the Cartographic History of North America, 1513–1930. A User's Guide,* for a comprehensive discussion of the evolution of the map of Texas during the nineteenth century.

2. David Weber, *The Mexican Frontier 1821–1846: The American Southwest under Mexico,* and id., *The Spanish Frontier in North America.*

3. D. W. Meinig, *Imperial Texas: An Interpretive Essay in Cultural Geography,* pp. 23–37.

4. See Ernest Wallace, *The Howling of the Coyotes: Reconstruction Efforts to Divide Texas.*

5. A definitive explanation of map projections is found in Frederick Pearson, *Map Projections: Theory and Applications.*

6. A detailed description of the Texas map in relation to GIS systems is found in a draft paper by Stephen Shackelford entitled "The Texas Statewide Mapping System: A Standard for Statewide Mapping."

7. Ibid., p.1

8. Kate Collins, conversation with author, Saint Monica's School, Dallas, Texas, Sept., 1992.

9. Townsend Miller, *A Letter from Texas* (Dallas: Nieman-Marcus, 1939), p.1.

10. Ron Henry, conversation with author, Fort Worth, Texas, July 11, 1992.

11. Roger M. Downs, "Maps and Metaphors," *Professional Geographer* 83 (1981): 287–93.

4: From Map to Symbol

1. Weber, *The Mexican Frontier,* pp. 242–72.

2. Robert A. Calvert and Arnoldo DeLeón, *The History of Texas.*

3. Meinig, *Imperial Texas,* p. 38.

4. Alan Gowans, *Learning to See: Historical Perspectives on Modern Popular/ Commercial Arts,* p. 462.

5. Ibid., p. 40.

6. Ibid., p. 70.

7. See Walter Prescott Webb, *The Handbook of Texas,* vol. II, pp. 585–86; and James Steely, "Texas' Lone Star," *Texas Highways* 36, no. 1 (Jan., 1989): 24–27.

8. This slogan was used in the late 1980s and early 1990s in advertising the *Texas State Travel Guide* in national magazines.

9. Bruce Neal, public relations director, Six Flags Over Texas theme park, conversation with author, Arlington, Texas, Sept. 16, 1992.

10. Carol Williams, curator, Fort Worth Cattleman's Museum, Feb. 24, 1992.

11. National Association of Chicano Scholars, 1992 Texas Foco Site Committee, open letter "to interested members of the Chicano community," n.d., 2 pp.

12. Terry Jordan "The Anglo-Texan Homeland," *Journal of Cultural Geography* 13, no. 2 (1993): 75–86.

13. James Steely, conversation with author, Toledo, Ohio, May 23, 1991.

14. Lazenby's development of this product is described in Harry Ellis, *Dr Pepper: King of Beverages,* centennial edition, p. 47.

15. Filewood, Yellow Pages survey, University of Texas at Arlington, unpublished research project, Sept., 1992.

16. Terry G. Jordan, "Perceptual Regions of Texas," *Geographical Review* 68 (1978): 293–307; and idem, with John L. Bean Jr. and William M. Holmes, *Texas: A Geography,* pp. 269–81.

17. Darwin Spearing, *Roadside Geology of Texas,* p.x.

18. Ron Henry, conversation with author, Fort Worth, Texas, July 11, 1992.

Epilogue: The Map of Texas and the Future

1. "Yellow Rows of Texas," *Fort Worth Star-Telegram,* July 13, 1994, sect. A, p. 15.

2. See, for example, two articles on the popularity of the Texas map: Anne Dingus, "Welcome Map," *Texas Monthly,* Statewide sect., May, 1993, p.88; and Jennifer Delson, "Texas Map Has Emotional Appeal, UTA Teacher Says," *Fort Worth Star-Telegram,* June 2, 1993, Northeast Sect. A, p. 17. The latter story was widely syndicated in Texas newspapers during the summer of 1993.

Bibliography

Calvert, Robert A., and Arnoldo DeLeón. *The History of Texas*. Arlington Heights, Ill.: Harlan Davidson, 1990.

Campbell, John. *Introductory Cartography*. Englewood Cliffs, N.J.: Prentice Hall, 1984.

Campbell, Tony. "Knowledge and Market Mechanism As Impulses for Map Publishing." In *Abstracts, XIII International Conference on the History of Cartography*, pp. 55–56, Amsterdam.

Dingus, Anne. *The Dictionary of Texas Misinformation*. Austin: Texas Monthly Press, 1987.

Downs, Roger M. "Maps and Metaphors." *Professional Geographer* 83 (1981): 287–93.

Downs, Roger, and Lynn Liben. "The Development of Expertise in Geography: A Cognitive Developmental Approach to Geographic Education." *Annals of the Association of American Geographers* (June, 1991).

Ellis, Harry. *Dr Pepper: King of Beverages*, centennial edition. Dallas: Dr Pepper Co., 1986.

Forman, Maury, and Robert A. Calvert. *Cartooning Texas: One Hundred Years of Cartoon Art in the Lone Star State*. College Station: Texas A&M University Press, 1993.

Francaviglia, Richard V. "Tex-Map Mania: The Outline of Texas As a Popular Symbol." *Journal of Cultural Geography* 12, no. l (fall/winter, 1991): 69–77.

Gowans, Alan. *Learning to See: Historical Perspectives on Modern Popular/Commercial Arts*. Bowling Green, Oh.: Bowling Green University Popular Press, 1981.

Graham, Don. "Texas Videos: The Best Texas Movies on Tape." *Texas Monthly* (July, 1991): 94–101.

Harley, J. B. "Deconstructing the Map." *Cartographica* 26, no. 2 (1989): 1–20.

———. "Text and Contexts in the Interpretation of Early Maps." Introduction to *From Sea Charts to Satellite Images: Interpreting North American History through Maps*, edited by David Buisseret, pp. 3–15. Chicago: University of Chicago Press, 1990.

Jordan, Terry G. "The Anglo-Texan Homeland." *Journal of Cultural Geography* 13, no. 2 (1993): 75–86.

——— "Perceptual Regions of Texas." *Geographical Review* 68 (1978): 293–307.

Jordan, Terry G., with John L. Bean Jr. and William M. Holmes. *Texas: A Geography*. Boulder, Colo.: Westview Press, 1984.

Kashgarian, Michael. "Garden Was a Tribute to Texas—Late Midlander Wiley W. Walls Planted Hundreds of Chinese Elms in the Shape of the Lone Star State." *Midland Reporter-Telegram,* October 17, 1993, pp. C2, 3.

King, Larry L. "Hollywood, Tx." *Texas Monthly* (July, 1991): 102–103; 128–30.

Lloyd, R. "A Look at Images." *Annals of the Association of American Geographers* 72 (1982): 532–48.

Marshall, Thom. "Stately Shape Y'all Know." *Houston Chronicle,* August 16, 1992.

Martin, Robert S., and James C. Martin. *Contours of Discovery: Printed Maps Delineating the Texas and Southwestern Chapters in the Cartographic History of North America, 1513–1930: A User's Guide.* Austin: Texas State Historical Association, 1982.

Meinig, D. W. *Imperial Texas: An Interpretive Essay in Cultural Geography.* Austin: University of Texas Press, 1969.

Monastersky, Richard. "The Warped World of Mental Maps." *Science News* 142 (October 3, 1992): 222–23.

Monomier, Mark, and George Schnell. *Map Appreciation.* Englewood Cliffs, N.J.: Prentice-Hall, 1988.

Muehrcke, Phillip C. *Map Use: Reading, Analysis, and Interpretation.* Madison, Wis.: J. P. Publications, 1986.

O'Donnell, Erin. "Deep in the Shape of Texas." *Esprit, the Magazine of the Mid Cities* 3, no. 3 (March, 1986): 40–41.

Pearson, Frederick. *Map Projections: Theory and Applications.* Boca Raton, Fla.: CRC Press, 1990.

Reinhartz, Dennis. "Greetings from the Lone Star State: Postcard, Cartoon, and Souvenir Maps of Texas." *The Map Collector* (spring, 1993): 24–28.

Reinhartz, Dennis, and Charles C. Colley, eds. *The Mapping of the American Southwest.* College Station: Texas A&M University Press, 1987.

Ristow, Walter. *American Maps and Mapmakers: Commercial Geography in the Nineteenth Century.* Detroit, Mich.: Wayne State University Press, 1985.

Robinson, Arthur H., and Barbara Bartz Petchenik. *The Nature of Maps: Essays toward Understanding Maps and Mapping.* Chicago: University of Chicago Press, 1976.

Robinson, Arthur H., Randall D. Sale, Joel L. Morrison, and Phillip C. Muehrcke. *Elements of Cartography,* 5th ed. New York: John Wiley & Sons, 1984.

Sanders, Leonard. *How Fort Worth Became the Texas Most City.* Fort Worth, Tex.: Amon Carter Museum of Western Art, 1973.

Schwartz, Maryln. "Feelings Go Deep for the Great State." *Dallas Morning News,* October 15, 1991.

Shackelford, Stephen. "The Texas Statewide Mapping System: A Standard for Statewide Mapping." Unpublished paper, Texas Department of Transportation, January 21, 1993.

Snyder, John P. *Map Projections—A Working Manual:* U.S. Geological Survey Professional Paper #1395. Washington, D.C.: U.S. Government Printing Office, 1987.

Spearing, Darwin. *Roadside Geology of Texas.* Missoula, Mont.: Mountain Press Publishing, 1991.

Steely, James. "Texas' Lone Star." *Texas Highways* 36, no. 1 (January, 1989): 24–27.

———. "THC Medallion Dates to 1961." *Medallion* 25, no. 10 (October, 1989): 1.

Tuan, Yi Fu. "Language and the Making of Place: A Narrative-Descriptive Approach." *Annals of the Association of American Geographers* 81, no. 4 (December, 1991): 684–96.

Vujakovic, Peter. "Comic Cartography." *Geographical Magazine* (June, 1990): 22–26.

Wallace, Ernest. *The Howling of the Coyotes: Reconstruction Efforts to Divide Texas.* College Station: Texas A&M University Press, 1979.

Webb, Walter Prescott, ed. *The Handbook of Texas.* 2 vols. Austin: Texas State Historical Association, 1952.

Weber, David J. *The Mexican Frontier, 1821–1846: The American Southwest under Mexico.* Albuquerque: University of New Mexico Press, 1982.

———. *The Spanish Frontier in North America.* New Haven, Conn.: Yale University Press, 1992.

Wood, Denis, and John Fels. "Designs on Signs: Myth and Meaning in Maps." *Cartographica* 23, no. 3 (1986): 54–103.

Wright, John K. "Map Makers Are Human: Comments on the Subjective in Mapping." *Geographical Review* 32 (1942): 527–44.

Zelinsky, Wilbur. "Where Every Town Is Above Average: Welcoming Signs along America's Highways." *Landscape* 30, no. 1 (1988): 1–10.

Index